a guide to
Finnish architecture

by J. M. Richards

FREDERICK A. PRAEGER

Publishers

New York · Washington

BOOKS THAT MATTER

Published in the United States of America in 1967
by Frederick A. Praeger, Inc., Publishers
111 Fourth Avenue, New York, N.Y. 10003

© 1966, J. M. Richards

Library of Congress Catalog Card Number: 67-25565

Printed in Great Britain

Contents

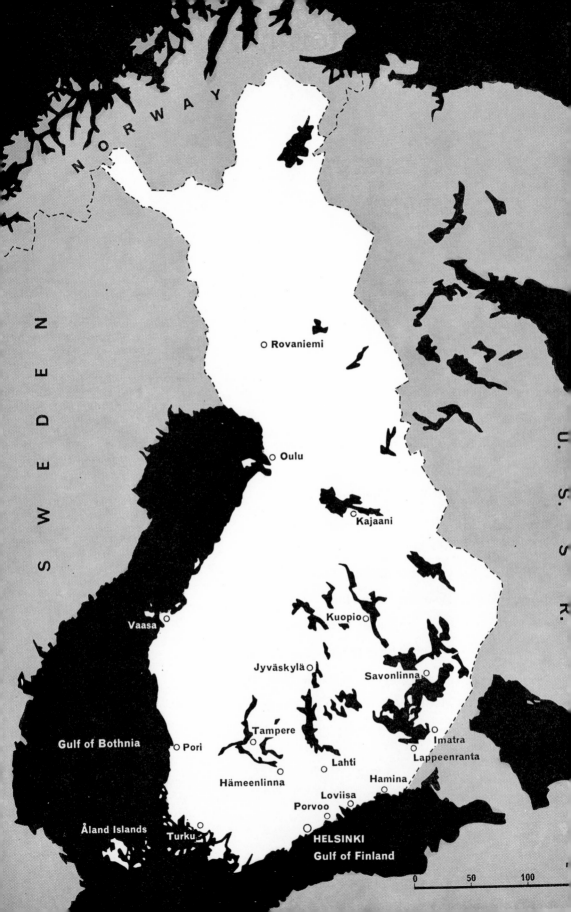

List of Illustrations

list of illustrations

To the memory of
Viljo Rewell (1910–1964),
with whom I first looked
at Finnish architecture

Foreword

THIS BOOK BEGINS WITH AN INTRODUCTORY ESSAY ON FINNISH ARCHI-
tecture and its special characteristics, after which each chapter deals with one
building type or period. In these chapters a preliminary text is followed by notes
on the most important or representative buildings, which are then shown in
photographs. The notes and the photographs are arranged as far as possible in
chronological order except in the last chapter, devoted to modern architecture,
where they are arranged under places and architects.

Most places in Finland have both a Finnish and a Swedish name. In these
pages the Finnish name is normally used, with the Swedish name added only
when it differs substantially.

About half the photographs in the book were taken by the author. For the
remainder, thanks are due to the Museum of Finnish Architecture in Helsinki,
to the publishers (K. J. Gummerus of Jyväskylä) of *Finland's Most Beautiful
Churches*, to the National Museum at Helsinki, to the town museum at Turku,
to the architects of some of the modern buildings illustrated and to the photo-
graphic files of *The Architectural Review*. An acknowledgement of the source of
each photograph is given on pages 101 and 102.

I Finland and its Architecture

ARCHITECTURE IS THE ART FOR WHICH FINLAND IS FAMOUS. THIS HAS been so for more than thirty years, during which time the Finnish contribution has been far greater than that of many more populated countries. Alvar Aalto's work has been one of the main international influences since before 1930, but Finland's recent fame is by no means due to him alone; there is a talented later generation which, while it looks up to Aalto as a master, is far from deriving all its ideas from him and has made its reputation on its own merits. In addition, whenever the earlier development of modern architecture, and the movements out of which it arose, are discussed other Finnish names – notably those of Sonck and Saarinen – are inevitably brought forward.

By way of contrast, the Finnish architecture of preceding centuries has largely been ignored, which is in a way natural since it has neither the seminal nor the spectacular qualities to be found in other European countries, Finland having been, for many of those centuries, only on the fringe of the civilized world; also, because of the predominating use of timber, many early buildings have not survived – the history of most Finnish towns is the history of a succession of disastrous fires.

Yet the earlier Finnish architecture deserves to be noticed, and several of its episodes – the building of village churches in the late medieval period, the achievements of Carl Ludwig Engel in the neoclassical style which transformed Helsinki, after about 1817, into the elegant city it still is, and the period of national romanticism at the end of the nineteenth century – made a unique contribution to architectural history and can be studied today in buildings that are distinguished even by international standards.

The aim of this book is to bring an account of modern Finnish architecture into the same perspective as that of earlier times and to link the two together; a logical process because the influences that have shaped Finland herself – her history, her climate and topography and the temperament of her people – are the common thread on which the story of all her architecture must be strung.

For a long while, as I have observed, Finland existed only on the fringe of civilization, and some of the characteristics of Finnish architecture derive from this – the absence of great monuments of the cathedral-building age (Christianity was established late and Finland was little influenced by Christian culture until long after the greatest era of medieval art; only the cathedral at Turku compares with the great Gothic structures that represented the power of the Church in other European countries), and the corresponding circumstance that the use of an architectural style employing the language of the renaissance only became general at the end of the eighteenth century when that language had almost run its course elsewhere in Europe and was there becoming either precious or debased.

Finland's history has, however, other characteristics from which the architecture that remains from her past derives more positive qualities. For example, unlike their Continental neighbours, the Finnish peasants were never serfs, and this is reflected in the self-sufficiency of the village community which was not, as in feudal countries, dependent on great houses or castles. There are no vast country mansions; the manor-houses – which exist in any case only in certain limited areas of the country – are modest in scale and pretension and the castles, instead of being also the residences of a landed aristocracy, are purely military fortresses.

In spite of her geographically remote situation Finland did not escape European dynastic rivalries and struggles for power; on the contrary, Finland was one of the meeting grounds of the West and the East, and the changes and conflicts this position involved is written into her history and visible in her architecture. Victory was most often with the West – or often enough at least to ensure that Finland was dominated by Western culture, arriving mainly by way of Sweden but to some extent from across the Baltic. Only parts of the Karelian provinces were subject, over the centuries, to strong Byzantine-Russian influences; Russian contacts with Finland generally were military rather than cultural. The obvious exception is the first few decades after 1809, when Finland became a Grand-Duchy of the Russian Empire and the flow of political, and to a lesser extent cultural, influence was from the east to the west; but even then, since the point of origin was St. Petersburg, and St. Petersburg (Peter the Great's 'window on the West') was the most European of Russian cities, Helsinki, which was rebuilt at this time, remained in style a Western capital.

There is only one sense, perhaps, in which the native Russian influence is visible in Finland: Finnish towns have much the same overall character as the towns of Sweden or north Germany except for the great breadth of the streets in relation to the height of buildings. Similar space-giving proportions are of course found in Canada and the western United States and other places where building in wood made it necessary to take precautions against the spread of fire, but a consistent townscape determined by such proportions is typically Russian and, in this way only, Finnish towns have a Russian aspect.

Finland's situation as a political – and for a large part of her history an actual – battleground has not only been responsible for the fragmentary nature of her architectural story over the centuries but has coloured her architectural aspirations right up to modern times. Her energetic pursuit of a national style around 1900 and her ready adoption of modern architecture in the 1930s can both be related to the Finns' self-awareness as a people able and anxious to control their own destinies as well as reflecting the dour self-reliant qualities of a nation that has always had to fight for what it has achieved.

In addition there is the influence of climate and topography. The visitor to Finland – especially if he goes there in winter-time (most tourists go in the summer, when they make the acquaintance of the less typical, though perhaps more superficially agreeable, aspects of Finnish life) – is soon made aware of the hard unrelenting nature of the country, which its architecture clearly reflects. I do not mean that there is any absence of beauty in the ice-bound coastline, or in the forested landscape in which primeval rocks lie very near the surface, or the lakes in which the ripples caused by the wind are fixed and frozen for months at a time. These add up to a picture, coloured grey and white and muted shades of brown, that has its own special beauty; and so has the summer-time picture, dominated by the green of forests and the changing blue and grey-blue of the endless waterways, and those who come to know the Finnish landscape develop a nostalgia for it that surprises them. But its beauty is of a kind that contains none of the exuberance, none of the sense of nature expending its superfluous energy, that we get in more southerly climates. In Finland nature and man must concentrate on holding their own.

This affects architecture in two ways: first it encourages a habit of persistent enquiry into technical possibilities – a search for new weapons with which to defeat and conquer the elements; and secondly, living so close to the more uncomfortable aspects of nature means that the essential relationship between the building, its materials and its setting is not easily lost sight of. This direct response to the forces of nature is the basis of the so-called organic quality that the great American architect Frank Lloyd Wright used to make so much of, and the work of Finland's outstanding modern architect, Alvar Aalto, exemplifies it strongly. Moreover, although the organic nature of the best Finnish architecture comes out so clearly in Aalto and those he has influenced – see Chapter 11 of this book, devoted to modern times – it is discernible also, along with a basic geometrical simplicity, in Finnish architecture of other periods.

But perhaps least in Helsinki, where most visitors get their introduction to Finland; because Helsinki, though now a capital city with all the metropolitan qualities, is comparatively a young city. Before the Russians made it the capital in 1812, after capturing Finland from the Swedes, it was a small and unimportant town with a population of only 4,000. Then it was laid out afresh, according to a plan previously drawn up by Johan Albert Ehrenström after a disastrous fire had almost wholly destroyed it in 1808. The architectural embodiment of the new plan was the handsome sequence of squares and public buildings by Engel described in Chapter 6.

They give a delightful consistency and formality to the centre of Helsinki, much as the Georgian squares and public buildings do to the centre of Dublin – another capital city to which Helsinki is in many ways comparable. Both possess the same seductive quality of light and the same clean-washed air that blows in from the sea, as well as the same arrangement of distinguished Government and university buildings set among the architectural flotsam and jetsam of a commercial port, along with the broad perspectives that belong to a port which is at the same time the gateway to a country.

Another parallel could perhaps be drawn between Helsinki and Dublin by relating the cultural and social stresses set up by the domination of the English minority over the native Irish to those resulting from the domination of the Swedes and those who spoke Swedish, during much of Finland's history, over the less worldly-wise and sophisticated Finns, though it is not a parallel that need be stretched too far. Helsinki and Dublin are moreover much the same size. The population of Helsinki has not quite reached half a million – an ideal size for a city of this kind; large enough to be fully metropolitan but small and compact enough for its central area to be covered on foot. It is to be hoped that, if the population must continue to increase, Helsinki will not be allowed to sprawl but will extend itself into self-contained satellite towns or use other planning devices that will preserve its shapeliness and comprehensibility. Tapiola, the beautifully designed dormitory town on the western fringe of the city, provides reassuring evidence that forethought is being exercised.

Helsinki, being in effect only a century and a half old, possesses no monuments of earlier date except the remains of the great eighteenth-century fortress of Suomenlinna on a cluster of islands in the harbour. Besides Engel's neoclassical buildings and a wide range of modern buildings of the last thirty years, the good buildings in which Helsinki is richest belong to the period of romantic nationalism that began soon after 1900 and is dealt with in Chapter 9. They were designed with remarkable conviction and a passionate belief in architecture's need to be rooted in local culture. Although the style was current for only a dozen years, while it lasted it dominated Finnish architecture in a way that occurred perhaps nowhere else. In other countries, although similar styles had their passing vogue and the *Art Nouveau* style in particular arose out of the same desire to escape from the strait-jacket of academic historicism, they represented the work of a minority of eccentrics and devotees. The earnest search for a new architectural idiom on the part of nearly all the leading Finnish architects between 1900 and about 1912 gives a fresh and surprising flavour to parts of Helsinki and other Finnish cities – parts built up when London, for instance, was hardly looking beyond the most conventional Edwardian Baroque.

Before the rebuilding of Helsinki the capital of Finland was Turku (Åbo in Swedish), and here isolated buildings do remain as evidence of the town's antiquity, notably the castle that commanded the sea approach to the town from a hill above the River Aura (the river that furnished the gateway through which European culture, and the Christianity that was its principal carrier, entered Finland) and the cathedral. The latter (see Chapter 3) is the one substantial building Finland possesses that can take its place among the Gothic cathedrals of Europe.

Around the cathedral and between it and the river is a charming group of neo-classical buildings dating mostly from the beginning of the nineteenth century (see Chapter 6), one of which was built for the first Åbo *Akademi*, the oldest university in Finland. In spite of having been replanned by the ubiquitous Engel after most of the town had been destroyed by fire in 1827, Turku is now, on the whole, a disappointing town; it has lost what character it used to possess as a result of recent central-area rebuilding in a commonplace and brashly modernistic style.

Tampere, Finland's second largest and leading industrial town, is more coherent and self-confident. Though founded in the eighteenth century, it is wholly modern in character and contains a number of distinguished recent buildings as well as a cathedral, finished in 1907, which is perhaps Lars Sonck's most important work. Towns, however, played a relatively small part in the early development of Finland, and in the other principal towns the architectural interest is likewise predominantly modern. In their visible form Finnish towns go back no further than a century and a half, though some were founded many years earlier – Pori (the Swedish Bjorneborg) in 1558; Vaasa in 1606; Oulu, in spite of being far to the north, in 1610; Kuopio in 1653. Porvoo (Swedish Borgå), on the Gulf of Finland east of Helsinki, which received its charter as early as 1346, is exceptional in preserving an old quarter fairly intact. Here narrow streets of wooden houses lead up to its fifteenth-century church and an eighteenth-century town-hall, now a museum, fronts on to a sloping cobbled square. Another unusual town is Hamina, still further east along the Gulf of Finland (in fact, since 1940, the last coastal town before the Russian frontier). It was rebuilt as a military centre in the eighteenth century and surrounded with fortifications and has a symmetrical radial street-plan forming a series of con-centric octagons with the town-hall in the middle.

Other towns possess perhaps a neoclassical church or a nineteenth-century town-hall, and in some instances (for example, Loviisa and Hämeenlinna) the remnants of a formal layout as reminders that they go back at least to the time of the Russian Empire, and most towns also have streets of wooden houses, perhaps no more than half a century old, of considerable charm, with fretted gables and ornamented window-surrounds (see Chapter 8). In the larger towns this vernacular wooden architecture is quickly disappearing.

If few Finnish towns possess buildings of much antiquity, in the villages medieval churches (see Chapter 3) are to be found in surprising numbers. About seventy of these survive, many with their original furnishings and wall-paintings. Other villages, especially in the south and west, have neoclassical churches built in wood by Engel or in the Engel style around 1820 or 1840. Whichever period they belong to, the village churches of Finland make a unique and too little known contribution to European architecture. They, together with the neoclassical buildings of Engel and his immediate predecessors, the buildings associated with the romantic movement of the beginning of this century and the buildings of the last twenty or thirty years, are those to which I have thought it right to give most attention in the following pages.

2 Fortresses

I USE THE TERM FORTRESSES RATHER THAN CASTLES TO INDICATE THAT in Finland the purpose of the buildings described in this chapter was almost wholly military, whereas in most other countries castles filled, in addition, the social role of residences of the nobility. The only exception among all the Finnish castles was that at Turku which, from the fourteenth century onwards, was the seat of the ducal court, and afterwards of the governor-general, but even in this case the purpose was administrative; the castle was never a family stronghold.

Finland is strewn with fortifications of a kind, having been so continually a battleground. The wars between the Swedes and the Russians, which were fought backwards and forwards across the Finnish countryside from the late sixteenth century until the early nineteenth, left behind great numbers of these, especially in the south-eastern region around Loviisa, Kotka and Lappeenranta, where the new frontier was fixed in 1721 after Finland (still then under Swedish rule) had been compelled – not for the last time – to cede to Russia parts of Karelia and the town of Viipuri.

But these fortifications and the others like them survive as little more than systems of trenches and embankments and lengths of stone revetment buried in the woods. In the early seventeenth century a castle was built at Kajaani in the remote northern country to defend the new settlements around the Oulujärvi lake, but it was destroyed a hundred years later, and in the eighteenth century the island of Svartholm, at the entrance to the Bay of Loviisa, was fortified, but little remains here either as a result of a British naval bombardment during the Crimean War.

The fortresses that survive as substantial works of architecture are limited to the three large medieval castles at Turku, Hämeenlinna and Savonlinna, to the lesser ones at Kastelholm among the Åland Islands and at Raasepori, and the eighteenth-century island fortress of Suomenlinna that guarded the approach to Helsinki from the sea.

Turku
Swedish Åbo
PLATE I

Built at the end of the thirteenth century, the castle of Turku stands on high ground commanding the harbour and the mouth of the river. It is visible from far out to sea. The oldest part consists of two parallel four-storey buildings separated at either end by six-storey towers, all in grey stone. The castle was improved in the fourteenth century by the addition of vaulted state banqueting halls and enlarged in the sixteenth century when the residential New Castle was added in the form of an outer courtyard on the slope of the hill. This housed the court of Duke John, one of the sons of the Swedish King Gustavas Vasa, and the castle was afterwards held by Klaus Fleming, the governor who rebelled against the duke-regent, the future Charles IX. Charles laid siege to it and captured it in 1599. In 1614, during a visit by Gustavus Adolphus, it was badly damaged by fire. After that it lost its military importance, though it was the residence of successive governors-general of Finland including the philanthropic Per Brahe who founded the Åbo *Akademi* in 1640. It was later used as a prison and since 1881 has been a museum. In 1941 its roofs were destroyed by bombing, but it has recently been thoroughly restored.

Savonlinna
PLATES 2–4

The castle of Olavinlinna (named after St. Olaf, patron saint of the Swedish nobleman and governor of Viipuri, Erik Axelsson Tott, who founded it in 1475) is one of the most romantically situated and best preserved in Scandinavia. It occupies a rocky island in the southernmost of the two lakes between which the town of Savonlinna, in eastern Finland, is set. It was intended for defence against the Russians, but after 1617 Finland's frontier was moved further east, too far away for the castle to play an important part in military operations. In 1714 and again in 1742 it fell into Russian hands and with the eventual conquest of Finland by Russia during the Napoleonic wars it lost its military importance. It became a civilian prison in 1847 and was later allowed to fall into decay. It was restored in the 1870s and again in recent years – a process that is still going on.

The original fifteenth-century castle had three circular corner towers (of which two survive) linked by ramparts enclosing a triangular stone-paved courtyard. Overlooking the courtyard was the rectangular Knights' Hall with living quarters below, and on the second floor of one of the towers was a stone-vaulted chapel. In the sixteenth century a larger

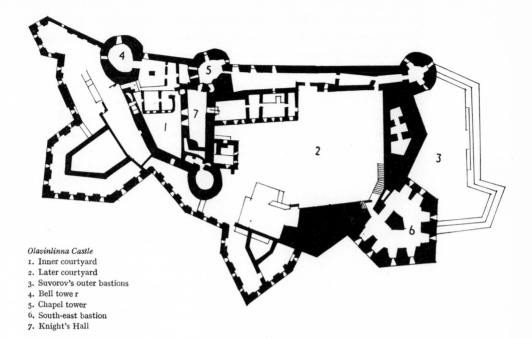

Olavinlinna Castle
1. Inner courtyard
2. Later courtyard
3. Suvorov's outer bastions
4. Bell towe r
5. Chapel tower
6. South-east bastion
7. Knight's Hall

courtyard surrounded by fortifications was added on the eastern side. These were protected by a circular keep at the south-east corner of the island, built in 1562, but this was destroyed in 1788 by the explosion of a powder-magazine and replaced by a lower bastion. Early in the seventeenth century another tower was built at the north-east corner, similar in style to the earlier ones, and this makes the third of the three circular towers that dominate the present castle from the outside. Their conical roofs date only from the end of the eighteenth century. At this time too the Russian General Suvorov made a number of additions including a series of outer bastions surrounding the castle.

Hämeenlinna
Swedish
Tavastehus
PLATE 5

The medieval castle of Häme is of the square type favoured by the Teutonic Knights and is built of brick (unusual in Finland) above a lower storey of stone. It stands on a hill north of the town, overlooking Lake Vanajavesi. The building dates mostly from the fourteenth and fifteenth centuries but is said to have been founded – by Birger Jarl – in the mid-thirteenth century. A round bastion (foreground of photograph) was added in the seventeenth century. The castle served until recently as a women's prison and is now being restored.

Suomenlinna
Swedish
Sveaborg
PLATE 6

This was a powerful system of fortifications occupying a group of islands in the harbour of Helsinki, designed to protect its seaward approaches. It was built by the Swedes in the 1750s and 1760s under the direction of Augustin Ehrensvärd, and because of its reputed invincibility it was known as the Gibraltar of the North. Nevertheless it surrendered to the Russians in 1808 without firing a shot, but it proved its strength later by withstanding the attack, during the Crimean War, of a joint British and French naval force. This bombardment (1855) destroyed the main headquarters buildings – a palatial governor's residence, officers' quarters, guardhouse, etc. – arranged in classical style round a courtyard. Little is left of other buildings and the fortress now consists of a richly romantic landscape of grass-grown mounds and bastions and stone-faced gun emplacements. It is entered, by way of a small landing stage, through the elliptical arched King's Gate, on the flanking walls of which are set tablets inscribed to commemorate the founding of the fortress. One of the inner bastions has had a summer restaurant installed within it (architect, Aulis Blomstedt). There are also a garrison church, a naval museum and Ehrensvärd's tomb.

1. Turku. The Castle (13th cent. and later).

2. Savonlinna. The island castle of Olavinlinna (15th cent. and later): from the mainland.
3. Castle of Olavinlinna: outer courtyard and bastion.
4. Castle of Olavinlinna: inner courtyard from the Knights' Hall.

5. Hämeenlinna. The Castle (14th cent. and later).
6. Suomenlinna (18th cent.): King's Gate.

3 Medieval Churches

CHRISTIANITY MAY BE SAID TO HAVE ESTABLISHED ITSELF IN FINLAND about 1229 when the first bishopric – later transferred to Turku and for centuries administering the whole country – was founded, though there had been earlier contacts with the Christian West. The Åland Islands, which now belong to Finland, had been Christianized and possessed stone churches with vaulted roofs as early as the beginning of the thirteenth century. The mainland was at this time a thinly populated – and indeed barely explored – wilderness, but following the so-called Crusades against Finland organized by the Swedes from the mid-twelfth century onwards by order of the Pope, Christianity spread up the river-valleys of the south-west and across the Häme region to Karelia. So energetically did Western culture penetrate the forests in its wake that by the end of the thirteenth century a number of the stone churches that today so splendidly enrich the Finnish rural scene had already been built, and many more, greatly influenced at first of course by Swedish models, were built during the fourteenth century. From that century also dates the cathedral at Turku.

The earliest village churches naturally arose in the extreme south-west, in the region around Turku. Among them was Nousiainen, where a bishop – the English-born Henry of Uppsala – had his seat even before the foundation of the bishopric of Turku. As stone-built churches spread to other parts of Finland, the different regions evolved their own characteristics. In the Åland Islands, for example, there was usually a western tower showing the influence of Gotland, an influence also to be found in Uusimaa, the southern region facing the Gulf of Finland, where there were many Swedish settlers. In Ostrobothnia, the flattish region bordering the Gulf of Bothnia, there were wooden churches, likewise showing Swedish influences (all Finland's medieval wooden churches have now disappeared). Typical of many parts of the south and west are gables faced with patterned brickwork, derived originally, it is thought, from north German and Danish sources.

The Finnish stone-built village churches are nevertheless characteristically themselves, with a strength and simplicity befitting their role of frontier posts of Western Christianity. The typical church is of the triple-aisled hall type, a plain rectangle in plan without the narrower choir of earlier date and without a tower. The walls are of undressed grey granite boulders. The nave is wider than the aisles but no higher. At the beginning there was often wooden barrel-vaulting, but stone-vaulted sacristies were added quite early, and in the fourteenth century brick (or sometimes stone) cross-vaulting became general over the whole church, followed in the fifteenth century by star-vaulting over certain areas such as the central aisle of the nave, the development of vaulting being of course influenced by the work going forward in Turku Cathedral throughout the fourteenth century.

These village churches are dominated externally by the great expanse of their shingle-covered roofs. There are usually two projections on the north and south sides: a sacristy and an armoury, the latter forming part of a south porch—see the plan of Hattula, page 29. There is an entrance in the centre of the west front, but not usually a window. The east end has a large window; the aisle windows are small but have in many cases been subsequently enlarged.

The brick decoration of the gables varies regionally; it may consist of groups of niches (said to symbolize, by their number, the Trinity, the twelve apostles and so on), perhaps a main niche in the form of a cross, or niches and recessed panels in various arrangements of vertical stripes, bands and circles. The recessed parts of the design are picked out with whitewash; in the past they may have been coloured. These decorated gables achieved their greatest elaboration at the end of the fifteenth century and the beginning of the sixteenth, when some churches had new gabled fronts added. Apart from the gables, the use of brick was limited to door and window surrounds, internal pillars and vaulting. The church at Hattula is a rare example of a fourteenth-century country church built almost wholly of brick.

A number of these churches – Inkoo, Kumlinge, Hattula and Lohja are perhaps the best examples – contain frescoes in a very good state of preservation, some as early as the end of the fourteenth century, and in several churches in the Åland Islands the end of the thirteenth. They were painted with a dry technique (as distinct from the familiar Italian technique in which the paint is applied to still-wet plaster), and in some cases – Lohja, for example, where the frescoes are early sixteenth century – the whole of the wall surfaces, together with the piers and the vaulting, are covered with an enchantingly fresh and flowing design of figures and foliage. In many churches the ribs of the vaulting are striped and patterned in terra-cotta red.

A characteristic feature of nearly all these village churches is the free-standing bell-tower, which is usually, however, of a later date than the church itself, having in the first place been built of wood and perhaps been several times replaced. Many bell-towers were rebuilt, again in wood, in the Engel (Russian Empire) period in a simple neoclassical style. Painted pale yellow or pale grey and white, they consort very happily with the grey stone, brick-gabled churches near which they stand in their tree-shaded graveyards, behind a foreground of granite tombstones, long grass and plant-tufted drystone boundary walls.

Hammarland
PLATE 7

Among the earliest of Finland's medieval stone churches are those on the Åland Islands. Hammarland is a village north-west of Mariehamn, the chief town of the islands. The church is thirteenth century and is unusual in having a choir rather narrower than the nave and a square tower at the south-west corner. Both the choir and the tower are a little later than the nave. The interior has stone vaulting, probably not constructed until the fifteenth century, with paintings (mostly floral scrollwork) of the same date.

Finström
PLATES 8 and 9

A short distance east of Hammarland is the somewhat larger church at Finström, late thirteenth century but on the site of an earlier wooden church. It is rectangular, with a small square sanctuary. The west tower is fifteenth century. With its shingle-covered spire and corner pinnacles, the church is typical of the Swedish churches of the time as well as of western Finland and Ostrobothnia (compare the later wooden churches described in the next chapter). The interior has fourteenth-century ribbed barrel-vaulting in natural stone, supported by double stone pillars, and fifteenth-century wall-paintings. Other medieval churches on the Åland Islands are at Eckerö (thirteenth century, with a tower resembling that at Hammarland), Kumlinge (see page 31), Jomala (parts of which are as early as twelfth century), Sund and Lemland.

Turku
Swedish Åbo
PLATES 10–13

The cathedral at Turku is the only major Gothic cathedral in Finland although some smaller medieval churches (for example, that at Porvoo), being the seats of bishops, have the title of cathedral. The two other principal cathedrals, though architecturally important, are of much later date: that at Helsinki (by Engel, 1830–52) and that at Tampere (by Sonck, 1902–07). These are described in Chapters 6 and 9.

Turku Cathedral is beautifully sited, just across the river from the modern part of the town, on a grassy mound with elegant neoclassical buildings of the beginning of last century grouped around it. Their pale smooth stucco walls serve as a foil to the cathedral's dark red pitted and textured brick, and the whole random complex of buildings is set among tall trees.

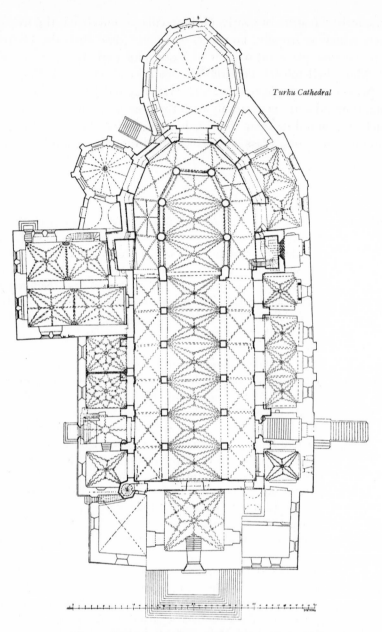

Turku Cathedral

The cathedral was first built about the middle of the thirteenth century (by Thomas, an English-born bishop) but was largely destroyed by the Russians in 1318. It was then rebuilt and enlarged in a style influenced by the churches of the Teutonic Knights on the other side of the Baltic. It was at this time (early fourteenth century) that the massive square western tower was built, to which corner turrets were added in mid-century; of the latter only traces remain. There was also a spire, later replaced by a curvilinear roof. This was destroyed by fire in

28

1827 and the present neo-gothic central turret was built in its place, bringing the total height of the tower to 300 ft.

The cathedral began as a triple-aisled hall-church, but in the fifteenth century chapels were added along either side of the nave and eventually combined to form, in effect, outer aisles – see plan. The side walls were subsequently raised and given clerestory windows, and new vaulting was built. In the middle of the fourteenth century a choir was added with octagonal pillars – those in the nave are square – and in the late fifteenth century an octagonal chapel at the east end. Also in the fifteenth century, the thirteenth-century sacristy at the north-east corner of the original church was enlarged and given a star-vaulted roof.

The length of the building today is 286 ft. and the width 127 ft. The side chapels contain a number of good monuments, mostly of the seventeenth century. The Tavast chapel (containing the remains of Magnus Tavast, a famous Catholic bishop of Turku who died in 1452) has a wrought-iron grille commissioned in 1425 by the bishop himself. Another famous bishop of Turku was Mikael Agricola (1508–57), who led Finland to adopt the Reformed (Lutheran) church and who first translated the Bible into Finnish.

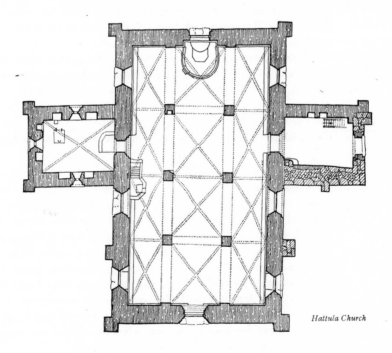

Hattula Church

Hattula

PLATES 14–16

This is a rare instance of a medieval church built mostly in brick. Being only a few miles north of Hämeenlinna it may have been influenced by the brick construction of Hämeenlinna Castle (see Chapter 2), which dates from about the same time – the early fourteenth century. Hattula church stands among fields in a walled enclosure entered on the north and south sides through brick and stone gateways that repeat on a smaller scale the geometrical form of the church. The north gateway only is contemporary with the church. On the west side is a bell-tower with a stone base and a nineteenth-century wooden superstructure.

The plan of the church, illustrated here, is that of most Finnish medieval churches: aisled rectangular nave with a sacristy projecting to the north and an armoury to the south. Hattula also has the typical very steep wooden roof. The walls are 5 ft. thick, of a double skin of brick, filled with earth. The west gable has a primitive version of the brick patterning developed more elaborately in later churches, in the form of a recessed cross flanked by niches. Apart from this decoration on the gables, external embellishment is rare in the Finnish medieval churches, but Hattula has six sculptured masks set high up in the wall. The interior has cross-vaulting and the vaults, the walls and the plain square pillars are covered with late fifteenth-century paintings, primitive in style but unusually delicate in colour. There are also some good sculptured figures in wood.

Tyrvää
PLATE 17

This is a small fourteenth-century village church of the usual hall type. It stands at the end of a peninsula projecting into a lake some miles to the west of Tampere and thus on the borders of Satakunta. The building, which has been out of use as a church since 1855, is notable for the unusual form of the brick decoration on the gables, which date from 1513–15. The east gable has a cross with circular ends subdivided into stars, surmounted by an arch of niches, and the west gable a stepped rectangular decoration enclosing a round-headed central niche. Inside there is wooden barrel-vaulting of the fourteenth century. The shingle roof, with its complex patterning, is an eighteenth-century replacement.

Isokyro
PLATE 18

This is one of the more northerly of the medieval stone churches, on the Kyrönjoki river between Lapua and Vaasa. Here Finnish troops, in bitterly cold weather, lost a decisive battle against the Russians in 1714. The early fifteenth-century church, which has been out of use since 1878, is shown in the photograph in its typical western Finnish setting near the edge of the water in a landscape of wide green fields.

The walls are of the usual grey stone, but the stone gables, being in bad condition, were replaced by wood boarding in 1820. Inside there are wall-paintings done in 1560 and thought, on the evidence of their style, to be by a north German artist. They were covered over in the seventeenth century but restored in 1720 when the church was repaired, its wood vaulting renewed and its windows enlarged.

Porvoo
Swedish Borgå
PLATES 19 and 20

The cathedral (for Porvoo is the seat of a bishop) stands on high ground in the centre of the old part of the town, shown in the photograph from across the river. It has the usual detached bell-tower, crowned by a two-tier curvilinear roof added in the eighteenth century. The church itself was built in 1414–18, but its sanctuary was widened and the vaulting added about half a century later. The central aisle has the star-vaulting that was coming into general use about this time. The east gable is filled by an elaborate brick decoration attributed to Carsten Nübuhr. The stone walls are otherwise limewashed, as is customary in this province of Uusimaa.

Pernaja
PLATE 21

The birthplace of the sixteenth-century Mikael Agricola (see under Turku Cathedral), Pernaja is an agreeable tree-planted village overlooking an inlet from the sea a short distance east of Porvoo. The church is late fourteenth century, and has fifteenth-century brick decorations on the west gable (very similar to those at Porvoo and perhaps therefore also by Carsten Nübuhr) and a brick-ribbed west doorway of about 1390. The brick vaulting, resting on cruciform columns, is fifteenth century, with star-vaulting in the central part of the three-aisled nave and arabesque paintings. There is a richly painted canopied pulpit of 1652, similar to the one in Turku Cathedral.

Hollola
PLATES 22 and 23

Standing high up above a rolling, well-farmed countryside, in a thickly planted graveyard which was once enclosed by a defensive wall, the church at Hollola, not far from Lahti, is one of the best preserved and embellished of the late medieval village churches. Its walls of uncoursed stone have a beautiful texture and subtly varied colour. It has the usual brick decorated gables and on the axis of the south porch a tall bell-tower reputedly designed by Carl Ludwig Engel though not built until 1848, eight years after his death. The bell-tower is so placed that the approach to the church is through the stone archway that forms its lower storey. Its upper storeys are of wood, painted pale yellow and white, and it terminates in a cylindrical domed cupola.

The church itself was built in 1480. It has a double-aisled plan with square brick piers carrying star-vaulting. The large armoury in its usual position on the south side is also vaulted. There is some good medieval ironwork (for example, the door from the armoury into the church) and figure sculptures in wood.

Rymättylä
PLATE 24

This is a single-aisled fourteenth-century church with fifteenth-century star-vaulting similar to that at Hollola. The village of Rymättylä is in the archipelago south-west of Turku. The walls of the church and the vaulting are covered with richly foliated paintings, done about 1520, showing renaissance influence.

Kumlinge
PLATE 25

This fifteenth-century church in the Åland Islands is one of the smallest of the medieval churches and is unusual in having a bell-tower over the armoury, which projects from the north side of the nave. This tower has a baroque spire added in 1767 by Antti Piimänen. The interior has a vaulted roof and sixteenth-century paintings.

Inkoo

PLATE 26

This church, in a village on the south coast, west of Helsinki, when first built in the thirteenth century was one of the earliest stone examples. It was enlarged in the fourteenth century and again at the end of the fifteenth – a period of very active church building in the province of Uusimaa. Inside it has vaulting (forming a double nave) similar to that at Hollola and medieval wall-paintings. The gable has a striking brick pattern employing a triple cross and groups of recessed rectangles and circles. The church shares a leafy rustic setting with a bell-tower of unusual form, consisting of a broad stone base and a three-tier wooden superstructure (eighteenth-century), each tier having a shingled roof.

Lohja

PLATES 27–29

This small town about 45 miles west of Helsinki has the largest of the medieval stone churches. It was built early in the fifteenth century and vaulted in the usual Uusimaa style in the late fifteenth century. Lohja is also one of the most remarkable of the medieval churches because of the paintings that cover the whole interior – walls, pillars and vaulting. They were done between 1514 and 1522. The church was restored in 1820, when the vicar made plans for drastically altering it and removing the paintings. His alterations were prevented, but the paintings were whitewashed over soon afterwards and not re-exposed until 1952 when they were found in good condition. They are a mixture of arabesques and groups of figures, lively and expressive and of beautiful colour.

Parts of the church are fourteenth century, but the nave and vaulting are fifteenth. It has the usual triple-aisled hall plan and is nearly 60 ft. high. The gable has brick decoration of comparatively simple design. The projected 1820 remodelling included a new bell-tower as the existing one was in bad condition, and a design was made by Engel (the drawings still exist). The parish, however, decided that the cost was too great, and restored the old one with a very simple wooden superstructure.

Siuntio

PLATE 30

This small village not far from Lohja has a modest specimen of the typical fifteenth-century grey stone church with round-headed windows inserted later, as was often done. Near the west end, but at an angle to it, stands a bell-tower with an early nineteenth-century wooden superstructure, painted grey and white, of a strange pagoda-like shape.

Pyhtää

PLATE 31

Another grey stone village church, between Loviisa and Kotka in the late medieval style typical of Uusimaa. It was built in the mid-fifteenth century and was clearly influenced by the church at Porvoo. It has the usual rectangular plan with three aisles, with star-vaulting over the centre one. The vaulting rests on cruciform columns – a shape only found here, at Pernaja and at Sipoo (which is between Helsinki and Porvoo). Pyhtää church retains its original brick-framed windows. Restoration in 1951 revealed wall-paintings of saints under the plaster, in a primitive style unique in Finland. Again the church has an unusual bell-tower, in this case with a square lower storey of whitewashed stone with a curved roof supporting an elegant octagonal wooden cupola.

7. Hammarland Church (13th cent.).

8

9

8. Finström Church (13th cent.; tower 15th cent.).
9. Finström Church: interior.
10. Turku. The Cathedral in its setting of trees and early 19th-cent. buildings.

11. Turku. The Cathedral (14th cent.): south side.
12. Turku. The Cathedral: western tower.
13. Turku. The Cathedral: interior looking east.

14. Hattula Church (14th cent.): with gateway.
15. Hattula Church: west end.
16. Hattula Church: interior (paintings 15th cent.).

15

17

18

24. Rymättylä Church: interior (wall-paintings 1520).
25. Kumlinge Church (15th cent.; spire 1767).
26. Inkoo Church (13th–15th cents.): bell-tower in foreground (wooden superstructure 18th cent.).

27. Lohja Church
(15th cent.).

28. Lohja
Church: bell-tower
(rebuilt 1820).

29. Lohja Church: interior (wall-paintings 1514–22).

30. Siuntio Church
(15th cent.) and
bell-tower (early
19th cent.).

31. Pyhtää Church
(15th cent.).

4 Later Churches – up to 1896

THE SEVENTEENTH- AND EARLY EIGHTEENTH-CENTURY CHURCHES, though serving the Lutheran instead of the Roman Catholic faith (Finland finally accepted the Reformation in 1527), remain largely medieval in conception. The sequence of stone-built village churches – Finland's most interesting contribution to medieval architecture – had come to an end and the new churches were of wood, but they followed at first much the same pattern as the wooden churches of the medieval period, none of which now remain. Architecturally in fact Finland emerged from the Middle Ages gradually and late.

In Ostrobothnia especially there was much church building in the seventeenth century, an activity which spread inland as more of the country acquired a permanent population. But medieval practices in the way of wall and roof construction and of vaulting persisted, as well as the medieval hall shape and, in some instances, the steep roofs and pinnacled towers. The first signs of a new approach to church design occurred in the second half of the century when centralized or cruciform churches – a renaissance rather than a medieval conception – began to appear, inspired it is generally presumed by St. Katherine's Church, Stockholm, designed by Jean de la Vallée in 1656.

From this new approach sprang the numerous cruciform churches – still built of wood – which by the late eighteenth century had become the commonest pattern in most parts of Finland, though there were other factors that led towards this plan shape besides the conscious adoption of the formal geometry of the renaissance. For example, a cruciform shape was arrived at, as in the case of Keuruu (1756–58), when the sacristy and armoury that projected on either side of the medieval type of church were transformed into a pair of transepts by

E

33

raising the level of their roofs. There were at the same time churches with polygonal eastern ends (a speciality of a leading master-builder, Matti Honka) that also seem to have developed directly from the medieval hall church. Finland being a meeting-ground of the Western and Eastern branches of the Christian Church, it might be supposed that the fashion for centralized church plans was a Byzantine one, due to Russian influence, but there is no evidence that this was so.

Whatever the origin of their new plan forms, and in spite of variations from region to region, the cruciform churches of the late eighteenth century – of which that at Purmo (1772) may be regarded as typical – increasingly conformed to sophisticated fashions in design, the more so as, at the end of the century, professional architects began to take over from the master-builders. One resulting development was the raising of a dome over the crossing, as at Lapua (1827) and Saarijärvi (*c.* 1830), and another was the introduction of variations on the basic cruciform plan which began with the practice of cutting off the angles, inside and out, and ended in some instances with polygonal plan-forms as at Vimpeli by Jacob Rijf (1807). In eastern Finland there evolved a double-cruciform type of church, the speciality of the Salonen family of builders, which may have influenced the ideas of some of the architects who designed neo-classical churches during the Empire period.

The internal arrangement of the churches also underwent changes in the course of the seventeenth and eighteenth centuries: the greater emphasis on the pulpit associated with the Lutheran religion had its influence, though the medieval choir-screen, an expression of Catholic mystery and ritual, survived in a modified form. Most of the screens were, however, destroyed in the nineteenth century. The practice of painting the walls and ceilings continued, often in the form of simulated architectural embellishments and draperies.

In the later seventeenth century the many-storeyed free-standing wooden bell-towers that are so characteristic a feature of the Finnish rural landscape first made their appearance. Some of them – those that stand alongside medieval churches – are described and illustrated in the preceding chapter because church and bell-tower are visually inseparable – the mottled grey stone walls of the church and the clear smooth colours of the bell-tower's paintwork are essential elements of the familiar village picture – but chronologically bell-towers belong to this chapter.

Like the village churches themselves, the bell-towers show variations in design from region to region. In Ostrobothnia, where the first bell-towers were built, the typical pattern has three storeys with an octagonal cupola, and there are similar patterns in the south-west (for example, Lohja and Siuntio already illustrated); in the south also, the main intermediate floor, which contains the bells, is sometimes octagonal and in eastern Finland there are late eighteenth-century examples, such as Ruokolahti, in which the whole structure, from top to bottom, is octagonal.

The wooden churches of this period, with their attendant bell-towers, are a remarkable series, unlike anything that other countries can show. Naïve and clumsy though some of them are in the handling of the renaissance idiom by the builders and master carpenters responsible for them, they yet have the freshness and directness of a true vernacular, a vernacular which was only gradually superseded by the individual architect-designed church, as the so-called Empire style (the style of the period, beginning in 1809, when Finland was a semi-autonomous Duchy of the Russian Empire) established itself.

This period, a period also of widespread civic building – see Chapter 6 – was dominated by Carl Ludwig Engel, but for some years before he came to Helsinki (that is, while Finland was still under Swedish rule) the leading architects, based on Turku, were already employing a similar late renaissance or neoclassical idiom. The work of these architects too is dealt with in Chapter 6, but their influence on church design falls within the scope of this chapter. The outstanding example is the church at Hämeenlinna, designed by Louis Jean Desprez in 1798. Though simple, and no doubt intentionally archaic, in its detail, this cruciform composition with a central rotunda and a tower crowned by a cupola, is, in spite of being an enlargement of an originally circular church, a fully realized architectural invention that owes nothing either to the improvisations of provincial carpenters or to the medieval traditions that had persisted in the Finnish countryside for so long.

The relative independence of Finnish church building practices from those prevailing in Sweden, in spite of Swedish political and cultural ascendancy, is underlined by the fact that Sweden had no central authority in charge of church building until 1759, and that even when such an authority had been set up its influence was limited to fostering a more academic attention to correct architectural style, resulting in little more than the incorporation of classical frontispieces in church elevations and the decorative application inside of classical elements like pilasters and wall panelling.

A Swedish statute of 1776 forbidding the use of wood for church building was but little observed, though a few stone churches – the first since the Middle Ages – were built towards the end of the century (Munsala and Kuopio are examples), and the practice of simulating the effect of masonry in the wall treatment of wooden churches may have been influenced by this official preference for stone.

Apart from a very few exceptions like the Desprez church at Hämeenlinna, and the work of another professional architect Jacob Rijf (for example his re-building, in a quite ambitious renaissance style, of a medieval church at Alatornio in 1794–97), the period of the architect-designed neoclassical church coincides with the early period of Russian Imperial rule. In 1810, the year after Sweden had yielded up Finland to Russia, a central building organization was set up in Finland. The first head of it – holder of the office of Controller of Public Works – was Carlo Francesco Bassi (see Chapter 6), an architect of

35

Italian origin, who designed a number of churches, a typical example being the Old Church in Tampere (1824). He was succeeded as Controller in 1824 by C. L. Engel, who had been working on the improvement and rebuilding of Helsinki since 1816.

Under Engel's supervision a great number of neoclassical churches were constructed and bell-towers in the same style were added to existing churches. He was in the fullest sense the architect of some of them, including metropolitan examples like the Vanha (Old) Church in Helsinki (1826) and the Lutheran cathedral (1830–40) which dominates the Government quarter of the city, and possibly some of the churches in important towns – important, that is, in his day – like Hamina and Lapua. Other churches built under his administration were no doubt the product of ideas and even of drawings issued by his organization; but many of the buildings to which the name of Engel is attached are unlikely to have been designed by him in any more direct sense, judging both by the sheer impossibility of one man producing so many designs in so short a time, and by the inexpert proportions and the unsophisticated, rough-and-ready details of the buildings themselves.

The Finnish churches of this period are nevertheless a remarkable achievement, and the presence, among the low wooden buildings of modest country towns, of ambitious domed neoclassical churches and many-storeyed bell-towers is an indication of the energy and administrative skill behind the architectural organization set up by the Imperial regime. This phase, however, lasted but a short time after Engel's death in 1840.

The later nineteenth-century Finnish churches fall into two main categories, the first of which is a direct continuation of what was being done a century before. It consists of wooden churches – they might be termed carpenters' churches whether in fact designed by master carpenters or by professionally trained architects – resembling the earlier wooden churches but deriving their architectural nature, inside and out, from their vigorous use of carpenter's ornament, often with a Gothic flavour, in the shape of applied pilasters, panelling and mouldings. The result is often somewhat gimcrack and nearly always naïve in relation to sophisticated standards of design; but these churches have a positive, idiosyncratic character and were sometimes surprisingly ambitious in scale, as in the case of the vast hill-top edifice at Kerimäki (1848), said to be the largest wooden church in the world.

The other category of later nineteenth-century churches conforms more closely to the eclectic fashions then being followed by architects elsewhere. Their work in Finland was especially influenced from north Germany, for although Finland continued to be a province of the Russian Empire until 1917, little architectural influence came from Russia except into the extreme eastern part of the country. Church architecture, as in other countries, was largely dominated by the Gothic Revival, and the neo-Gothic church at Pori (1863) by G. T. Chiewitz, illustrated here, may be taken as typical of this period. It led on, at the end of the century, to the more vigorous and inventive National Romantic style, which is separately dealt with in Chapter 9.

Tornio
PLATES 32 and 33

The small town of Tornio, a timber shipping port, lies right on the Swedish border at the head of the Gulf of Bothnia, on an island in the river, connected to Sweden by a spit of land and to Finland by a bridge. The church, which has been out of use since 1735, is a remarkable wooden structure with the steep shingle-covered pointed roofs typical of Ostrobothnia. Though built (by the master carpenter Matti Härmä) in 1684–86, it is still in many ways medieval in conception. Inside it has a vaulted wooden ceiling richly painted with wreaths enclosing circular panels with saints and angels, and a choir-screen and other furnishings carved in 1706 by Nils Fluur, a native of Tornio. The painter was the Danish-born Didrik Möllerum. The bell-tower, the oldest in north Finland, was built in 1687.

Lemi
PLATE 34

A modest village church, built in 1786, of full cruciform shape (that is, with the transepts the same height as the nave), a small cupola over the crossing and an elaborately patterned shingle roof. The ladder seen in the photograph is a permanent fixture in these wooden churches as a precaution against fire. Lemi is in south-east Finland, between Hamina and Lappeenranta, and the similarity of this church to that at Purmo, illustrated next, shows how, by the late eighteenth century, the style of design developed in Ostrobothnia had spread across the country as far as Karelia.

Purmo
PLATE 35

This is a rather more sophisticated version of the church at Lemi, described above, being situated further west on the edge of the Ostrobothnian plain. It was built in 1772 and has the same cruciform plan and central cupola. Its three-tiered bell-tower is typically Ostrobothnian.

Nurmo
PLATE 36

The bell-tower here is almost identical with that at Purmo, with only minor variations in detail, showing how near-standard designs were evolved, presumably by one master carpenter, and used in places quite a long way apart – Nurmo is just south of Lapua. The bell-tower stands right on the village street. Note in the photograph, attached to its base, one of the carved wooden costumed figures (*vaivaisukko*) holding a collecting-box for the poor that are found in many of these Ostrobothnian churches. The church itself (late eighteenth-century) follows the familiar pattern, with a somewhat more elaborate central cupola over an octagonal structure created by cutting across the internal corners of the basic cruciform plan.

Lappeenranta
PLATES 37 and 38

This is an Orthodox church, one of the few included in this survey, the Greek Orthodox rite being in the main confined to Karelia and other parts of eastern Finland, which have been perennially under Russian rule and, because of their nearness to Russia itself, always under Russian influence. Lappeenranta, by the Treaty of Turku signed in 1743, after a Finno-Swedish army had been heavily defeated in a battle near by, became Russian territory and a fortified frontier town. To the north-west of the town are the remains of fortifications built at this time, and the plain but elegant church, entered through an attached bell-tower, stands among them.

It was built in 1785 and has a simple plan with a barrel-vaulted nave separated from flat-ceilinged aisles by pairs of columns, but the white and gilt interior is given great richness by baroque furnishings and by the gilt-framed paintings displayed all over the walls as well as over the solid screen which, as in all Orthodox churches, hides the sanctuary from the nave.

Munsala
PLATE 39

A church of cruciform plan with attached western tower, in a village on the Gulf of Bothnia, north of Vaasa. Its design, made in 1777 by C. F. Adelcrantz, marks the first use of stone for the building of churches since the medieval stone churches of the fourteenth and fifteenth centuries; also the use of a fairly sophisticated renaissance idiom imported from Sweden.

Kuopio
PLATE 40

This is another stone church (now with the title of cathedral, since Kuopio is the seat of a bishop), similar to Munsala and built in 1815.

Hämeenlinna
Swedish
Tavastehus
PLATES 41 and 42

Hämeenlinna is a mature medium-size town 60 miles north of Helsinki, notable among other things for being the birth-place of Sibelius. The church was built in 1798 and was designed by Louis Jean Desprez, an architect of French origin who worked in Sweden. It is a handsomely modelled stucco-faced building with simple somewhat archaic detail,

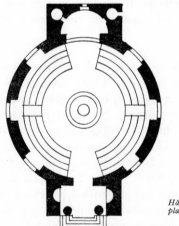

Hämeenlinna Church:
plan before enlargement

precociously Greek in places – for example, the columned porch facing the market square. This was part of the church as first built. It was then circular in plan, with the seating arranged round a central altar, and was modelled on the Pantheon at Rome. This was at the suggestion of King Gustav III of Sweden, who came back from a visit to Italy with a project to commission churches of the Pantheon type in Sweden and Finland, but the church at Hämeenlinna was the only one built. The tower and cupola were added in 1837 and the church was enlarged, by Josef Stenbäck, in 1892 to give it its present cruciform shape.

It stands up conspicuously, within a tree-planted enclosure, at the upper end of Hämeenlinna's sloping market square – the formal centre of the town; see Plate 78.

Helsinki

PLATES 43–45

With the Vanha (Old) Church (Plate 43) we approach the golden age of Finnish civic architecture, when Carl Ludwig Engel adorned Helsinki, after it had become the capital under the new Russian regime, with the formally laid out neoclassical buildings that give so much distinction to the city's Government area – see Chapter 6. This church, designed by Engel in 1826, before he began the cathedral, stands somewhat apart from his main group of civic and university buildings, of which the cathedral is the centre, since it is on the further side of the central avenue formed by the tree-lined Esplanade and Mannerheimintie, though near their junction. It occupies one corner of a green space between Lönnrotinkatu and Bulevardi and is a good example of Finnish wooden church architecture at its most assured and dignified. It is now much used for ceremonial purposes.

The Lutheran Cathedral (Plates 44 and 45; also Plate 70) was designed by Engel and built between 1830 and 1840. It dominates Senate Square and the whole Government and university area – see Chapter 6 – and indeed the city itself when approached from the sea.

Helsinki Cathedral

It stands at the top of a wide flight of steps at the upper end of the sloping square, the steps being terminated at either end by tall pedimented pavilions, bteween which a high platform runs across the front of the cathedral's southern portico. A similar flight of steps, facing the University Library, leads up to the western portico. The main flight of steps (replacing a colonnaded guardhouse), the corner pavilions, the four small domes surrounding the drum of the main dome and the zinc statues of the twelve Apostles above the main cornice (whose dark colour, together with the blue colour of the domes, give extra liveliness to the building's skyline) were all added in the 1840s, just after Engel's death. Though the building was completed in time to be used, only a few months after his death, to celebrate the bicentenary of the founding of the university, it was not in fact consecrated until 1852. The interior, with its large saucer dome (restored in 1962), is relatively plain and academic.

Lapua
PLATE 46

In the centre of Ostrobothnia, Lapua has been the scene of many important events in Finnish history, political and military. A river, the Lapuanjoki, flows through the town, and beside it stand this large domed wooden church by C. L. Engel (or the Public Works office controlled by him) and its characteristic three-storey bell-tower. The office designed, from 1820 onwards, a number of churches of similar type, but that at Lapua was the first to be completed, in 1827. It has a cruciform plan with a high central octagon and octagonal dome.

Saarijärvi
PLATES 47 and 48

A village church resembling that at Lapua and presumably only a few years later, but with a true dome instead of an octagonal domed roof, crowned by a cylindrical cupola, and with a more elaborately architectural bell-tower. There are balconies across each transept, alternately recessed and projecting, which create in the interior an unexpectedly baroque feeling. The village is 50 miles north-west of Jyväskylä.

Hamina
Swedish
Fredrikshamn
PLATE 49

The Orthodox church occupies one of the angles formed by the radiating streets of this remarkably laid out town – see Chapter 6. It is a circular domed building of 1837, in a walled enclosure which is entered through the arched lower storey of a free-standing bell-tower. This has a somewhat fanciful upper storey with steeple and miniature onion dome which give it an appropriately Russian flavour although it was in fact designed by an Italian architect called Visconti. The combination of its green roofs and pink and white paintwork gives the group of buildings, standing among trees, a toy-like prettiness.

Rautalampi
PLATES 50 and 51

Another typical wooden church of the Empire period, attributed to Engel but dated three years after his death, and clearly more a product of the office he controlled than of his own pencil because of its strange proportions and inexpert handling of detail. The church is of considerable size for a mere village, and over the west door is a tablet with an inscription recording that it was built in 1844 on the orders of the Czar Nicholas I. The three-storeyed bell-tower has a simple rustic charm. Rautalampi is in central Finland between Kuopio and Jyväskylä.

Karhula
PLATE 52

This small town is an industrial adjunct of Kotka and contains, among other installations, Alvar Aalto's Sunila wood-pulp factory (see Chapter 10). The church, built in 1850, is a more expert and professional equivalent of the provincial wooden churches already noted, providing a stylistic link between them and the architect-designed churches of the latter part of the century. Like the former it has a cruciform plan. It is built of stone, except for the upper storeys of the attached bell-tower.

Kerimäki
PLATES 53 and 54

This is perhaps the most extraordinary wooden church in Finland. It is of vast size (it claims to be the largest wooden church in the world, and it may well be so; its most likely rivals being the cathedral at Georgetown, Guyana, and the Mormon Tabernacle of 1870 at Salt Lake City with its vast elliptical roof). Kerimäki Church stands on a hilltop in the rolling landscape of eastern Finland, about 15 miles east of Savonlinna, so that its somewhat ungainly outline can be seen for miles. Kerimäki is only a village – though one that serves as the centre of a large rural area – yet the church seats 3,400 people. It was first plannned in 1842 by E. B. Lohrmann to seat 1,500, but the parishioners demanded something larger and A. F. Granstedt (who had been one of Engel's official assistants) was commissioned to provide an enlarged version of the Lohrmann design. The construction was the work of the parishioners themselves, the only trained craftsman being the builder in charge, and this no doubt explains the odd variations in scale and the naïve application of a mixture of classical and Gothic detail. The style as a whole, as well as the cruciform plan, closely resembles that of the mid-century carpenters' churches referred to above.

Kerimäki church was completed in 1848. The interior is much more successful than the exterior, the sense of space being truly impressive, the lighting well controlled and the ornament more subtly handled. What might appear a somewhat clumsy use of wooden struts and tie-beams in fact adds to the scale and interest of the upper spaces, especially the space, clerestory lit, beneath the central dome. The colour of the interior is also excellent, with light grey paint reinforced by marbling on the columns and pilasters.

Kajaani
PLATE 55

This is a typical instance of the tradition of carpenters' churches being carried on by the professional architects. Built as late as 1896, by J. Ahrenberg, it has a wholly consistent interior, all in wood, with columns, boarded ceilings and hammer-beam roof as well as a full complement of furniture: pews, north gallery and pulpit are shown in the photograph. The style, as one would expect so late in the century,

F

is more Gothic than in the earlier carpenters' churches, with evidence of German influence.

Kajaani is an industrial town on Lake Oulujärvi in north central Finland, on the main road leading up to Lapland. The town was founded by Per Brahe in 1651. It, too, has a town-hall (1831) attributed to Engel; also the ruins of a castle – see Chapter 2.

Pori
Swedish
Björneborg
PLATE 56

Pori is an ancient town on the Gulf of Bothnia from which the sea has now receded. It has a geometrical plan, the result of systematic rebuilding after a series of destructive fires, the last in 1852, and a town-hall by Engel, built in 1841. The church, which stands by the bridge across the Kokemäenjoki, exemplifies the historical revivalism that was current all over Europe at the time it was built – 1863 – but it also retains something in common, notably in its angular Gothic detail, with the carpenters' churches still being built in Finland, in spite of the spire and window-frames being in this case of cast-iron – the only example in Finland of the use of this material for such purposes.

The architects were G. T. Chiewitz and C. T. von Heideken. Chiewitz was a leading architect around the middle of the nineteenth century. He first practised in Sweden and came to Finland in 1851, where his most important building was the House of the Nobility in Helsinki (Plate 88). In 1860 he became town architect of Turku, but he died two years later. von Heideken, who completed the church after Chiewitz's death, was also the architect of Tjusterby manor-house (Plate 61).

32. Tornio Church (1684–86; bell-tower 1687).

33. Tornio Church: interior (furnishings 1706).

48. Saarijärvi: the bell-tower.

49. Hamina. Orthodox Church and bell-tower (1837).
50. Rautalampi Church (1844).
51. Rautalampi: the bell-tower.

5 Manor-Houses

FINLAND, AS THE OPENING CHAPTER OF THIS BOOK EXPLAINS, HAS NEVER been a country of feudal castles and aristocratic mansions, and country houses of a more modest kind were relatively few. The earlier examples, built of logs, were little different from farmhouses, and while the rest of northern Europe was cultivating, from the seventeenth century onwards, a form of civilization based largely on country house life and the power that resided there, Finland built few such houses of any architectural pretension. Louhisaari (1655), near Turku, is one example that survives of the square symmetrical renaissance-style mansion; others are Sarvlax, illustrated here, and Degerby at Loviisa. These, it may be noted, are in regions primarily Swedish in language and allegiances.

Even such aristocratic or manorial life as there was vanished in the eighteenth century when Finland was torn by wars and occupied by Russian troops, and the Swedish nobility who owned estates there were recalled to Sweden by royal command. Not till the end of the century, when conditions became more settled, were country houses built again, this time chiefly for the merchant class; the Swedish aristocracy did not, except in a few areas, re-establish itself on the land. The leading architect who specialized at this time in country houses was the German-born C. F. Schröder, who worked in Turku. Among the mansions he designed was Fagervik, in the southern province of Uusimaa.

There was a second period of country-house building at the beginning of the nineteenth century. Carlo Francesco Bassi, the Italian-born architect who was Finland's first Controller of Public Works, designed a number, and his successor, Carl Ludwig Engel – the dominating architectural figure of the Russian regime that began in 1809 – was nearly as prolific in his output of country houses as he was in that of town-halls and churches. These were seldom, however, on the palatial scale of the great country houses built elsewhere in Europe, the only Finnish mansion that compared with even the lesser of these being Mon Repos, a wooden neoclassical mansion designed by Engel in a landscaped park outside Viipuri – and thus no longer in Finland. Otherwise the Finnish country houses, which are nearly all of wood and are mostly to be found in southern and western Finland, especially in the traditionally Swedish-speaking areas, are best compared with the Queen Anne or Georgian mansions of country squires in England, being relatively modest in scale and serving also as the administrative centre for large agricultural estates.

Sarvlax PLATE 57	This is one of the few surviving seventeenth-century manor-houses and is in an excellent state of preservation, having been well restored at the end of last century. It was built in 1619. It is a four-square three-storey building, with pilasters from ground to cornice round all four sides and a small central pediment front and back. It is approached axially through a gravelled forecourt with parterres, etc., enclosed immediately in front of the house by low outbuildings on either side. The photograph shows the garden side. The loggia is a later addition. Sarvlax is near the village of Pernaja, just east of Porvoo, and in the graveyard of Pernaja church (see page 31) stands a sepulchral chapel belonging to the Creutz, von Morian and von Born families, successive owners of the Sarvlax estate. This is a handsome Greek Revival structure of 1834, designed by Pehr Granstedt.
Fagervik PLATE 58	Like Sarvlax, Fagervik (which is near the south coast, west of Helsinki) has a formal layout on the entrance side with low flanking buildings enclosing a forecourt. It was designed by C. F. Schröder, a German-born architect from Turku, and completed in 1773. It is all built of wood, with a three-storey centre pavilion and two-storey wings with an additional storey in a mansard roof. It stands close by the edge of a lake, forming a group with its own estate buildings and – also at the water's edge – a cruciform wooden church of 1737 and its bell-tower of 1766.
Viurila PLATE 59	A simple pedimented three-storey country house by Carl Ludwig Engel, built in 1840. It is near Salo, between Turku and Helsinki.
Vuojoki PLATE 60	This was one of the largest country houses designed by Engel and consists of a main three-storey block flanked by single-storey pilastered pavilions, the latter being in line with the main block instead of being –

as in the case of the earlier manor-houses – brought forward to enclose an entrance courtyard. The house was completed in 1836 and is in southern Ostrobothnia, just north of Rauma.

Tjusterby
PLATE 61

This manor-house is unusual in several ways: for its late date (1867) and for being built of red brick, in a romantic style with a Gothic flavour. It was designed by C. T. von Heideken – a pupil of Chiewitz, for whom he completed the church at Pori (see page 41). It is not far from Sarvlax, near the village of Pernaja, and stands in a beautifully wooded estate of some antiquity, containing farm buildings dating back to the early eighteenth century.

57. Sarvlax Manor-House (1619).

58. Fagervik Manor-House. C. F. Schröder (1773).
59. Viurila Manor-House. C. L. Engel (1840).
60. Vuojoki Manor-House. C. L. Engel (1836).

former year it was severely damaged by a fire nearly as disastrous as that at Turku. Rebuilding plans were drawn up by a Lieutenant Kocke, but before these could be carried out the decision was taken to make Helsinki the new capital and new plans were made, of a more revolutionary and far-sighted kind, on the orders of the Czar Alexander I, said to be with the object of exhibiting the magnanimity and the civilizing intentions of the new regime.

The author of the new town plan, which was finalized in 1817, was Johan Albert Ehrenström, a politician and amateur of the arts, who presided over the reconstruction committee during fourteen years. His plan was grand in scale and classical in conception and central Helsinki as it appears at present, with the wide Esplanade running westwards from the south harbour and the spaciously laid out squares and terraces of monumental buildings climbing the slope to the north, and dominated by the cathedral, derives from it. The predominantly three-storey buildings in the centre gave way to lower wooden buildings in the surrounding residential quarters, all likewise neoclassical in their proportions and details, set among gardens as they became more widely spaced at the outer edge of the city.

Helsinki has been continuously extended, modernized and rebuilt, but the central area of 1817–40 remains virtually intact and furnishes some indication of the marvellous sight it must have afforded a century and a half ago: a model city, all of a piece in its layout and its architecture, light in tone since it was wholly of painted wood and stucco, expertly set into its rocky landscape penetrated by arms of the sea, ice-bound or in sparkling movement according to the season. Its creation was a remarkable achievement in that time and place, and in the space of a single generation.

The achievement as we now see it lies, however, not so much in Ehrenström's plan which, though far-sighted and ambitious, was a conventional product of its time, as in the architecture by Engel that gave it three-dimensional form. Ehrenström's great service to Finland was the invitation, issued to Engel by him and his reconstruction committee in 1815, to come to Helsinki from St. Petersburg and take architectural control of the new capital. Carl Ludwig Engel (1778–1840) was German by origin. He was a fellow student of Schinkel, and studied in Italy as well as in Berlin. He had worked for some years first in Reval and then in St. Petersburg before coming to Finland (where he stayed for the remainder of his life – another twenty-five years), and the influence of St. Petersburg is clearly evident in the design of several of his buildings in Helsinki, superimposed on the style of design associated throughout central Europe with the name of Schinkel. This is especially so in some of his earlier ones like the guards' barracks in Kasarmi Square with their crisply modelled surface decoration, and the inspiration of St. Petersburg is seen as well in his skilful subordination of the architectural features to the unity of the whole.

Engel succeeded Bassi as Controller of Public Works in 1824, by which time he had already completed a number of buildings in central Helsinki. These

included the Senate House (1818–22), which forms the eastern side of the monumental Senate Square. The Lutheran cathedral, on its high platform (see Chapter 4) occupies the northern, or upper, end of the square, and after the university
had been moved from Turku to Helsinki in 1828, Engel designed the main
university building (1828–32) on the west side of the square and the university
library (1836–44) alongside it to the north and therefore facing the west side of
the cathedral. North of the library again was the Russian military hospital, now
part of the university hospital and medical school.

Engel designed many other public buildings in Helsinki, including the Old
Church (Plate 43), the city hall (1833) facing the south harbour, the guards'
barracks already mentioned (1825) of which only one block survives, the remainder having been destroyed by bombing in the last war (see page 87), naval
barracks, hospitals and the buildings in Unioninkatu and Aleksanterinkatu that
now house the municipal offices and the law courts. He, or the office he controlled,
also produced formal plans for a number of Finnish towns which they embellished with town-halls and other civic buildings. Pori, Lappeenranta, Kajaani
and Kokkola have town-halls to which Engel's name is attached, and he was also
responsible for the observatory (1818) at Turku, the central part of the old
grammar school at Kuopio (1825) and the museum at Tampere (originally a
Government granary). Some of the numerous churches designed by him and his
office, and the part they played in the evolution of Finnish church architecture,
were described in Chapter 4.

One other Helsinki architect should be mentioned in connection with civic
buildings: Pehr Granstedt, who designed the President's palace, formerly the
Czar's Helsinki residence, in 1818. This is another, somewhat plain, neoclassical
building with a central pediment supported on columns. Facing the south
harbour it forms, with Engel's city-hall already referred to, and several later
buildings (see Plate 76), a continuous architectural wall that furnishes both a
dignified background to the bustle of the market square and, in the more distant
view, a base to the sequence of monumental buildings, crowned by the cathedral,
climbing the slope behind.

Porvoo	The old town-hall, built in 1764, occupies one side of a cobbled square
Swedish Borgå	in the old part of the town not far from the medieval church – see
PLATE 62	Plates 19 and 20. The main façade is colour-washed in terra-cotta, with
	details picked out in white. In this building the first Finnish diet met in
	1809 to proclaim the union between Russia and Finland – never, how-
	ever, to be summoned again until 1863 – see page 63. The building is
	now a museum, with admirably arranged rooms illustrating local life
	and history.

Hamina
Swedish
Fredrikshamn
PLATES 63–65

This is the last coastal town on the Gulf of Finland before the Russian frontier, which lies 28 miles to the east. The earlier town on the site was destroyed during the Russian occupation of 1713–21, but was rebuilt after the Treaty of Uusikaupunki (Swedish Nystad), signed in 1721, which ceded parts of eastern Finland to Russia, making Hamina a frontier town. It was then fortified. After the 1741–43 war it became Russian territory again and remained so until the whole of Finland became a Russian Grand-Duchy in 1809 – in fact for three years longer, since the ceded territories were not reincorporated in the Duchy until 1812.

It was during the period of fortification by the Swedes, after 1721, that Hamina was given (by Carl A. Blaesingh) its geometrical street layout, consisting of a series of concentric octagons linking the streets that radiate from an octagonal central place – a layout that still exists, though it is not so evident on the ground as it is in the aerial view because the varying heights of buildings, and certain cleared spaces, make its symmetry incomplete.

In the middle of the central octagon stands the town-hall, a rectangular pedimented building of 1798, with an octagonal tower and two-stage turret added by C. L. Engel when he restored the buildin~ in 1840, after one of those destructive fires of which Finnish tow~ were so often the victims. On the north-west side of the square is

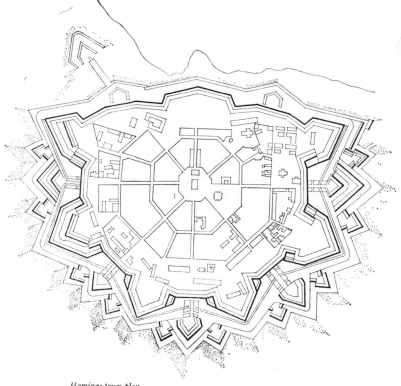

Hamina: town plan

Lutheran church (also by Engel), a plain rectangular building without a tower, completed in 1843; on the opposite side is the Orthodox church in its tree-planted compound (see page 40) – also seen in the photograph of the town-hall – and further to the east is the reserve officers' training school whose main building is illustrated on Plate 91. Near the market square, which lies to the west of the town centre, is a charming octagonal two-storey building – the so-called Flag Tower – with a curvilinear roof. It was constructed in 1790 on one of the bastions of the fortifications.

Turku
Swedish Åbo
PLATES 66–69

The Old University building (1802–15) was designed by Carl Christoffer Gjörwell under the supervision of C. F. Bassi, who was later to become Turku's leading architect and Finland's first Controller of Public Works. It was the first of Turku's group of neoclassical civic buildings, and with its plain wall surfaces unbroken by columns or pilasters, and its general severity of style, it presents something of a contrast to the style evolved in the decades that followed, by Bassi and P. J. Gylich in Turku and by Engel in Helsinki. It has a central assembly hall with columns of polished red granite and an elaborately ornamented vaulted plaster ceiling. The hall is flanked by open courtyards. The building stands just to the south of the cathedral and now houses the Appeal Court and various local government offices. The assembly hall is used for concerts.

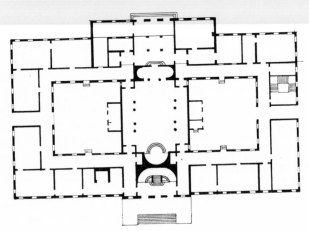

Old University Building: Turku

The main building of the present Åbo *Akademi* (the Swedish-language university) stands to the west of the old one and was formerly the residence of the Trapp family. It was designed by Bassi in 1832–33. Further to the left in Plate 68 is another house, of about the same date, by Gylich. Plate 69 shows another of the buildings (probably also by Gylich) around the cathedral. It was built in 1829–31 and houses one of the faculties of the Åbo *Akademi*. It is shown also in Plate 19,

The main part of Turku is on the opposite side of the River Aura from the cathedral. Here a new town was laid out by C. L. Engel after the fire of 1827. Its focal point is the Market Square (Kauppatori) where two main streets intersect. On the west side of the square is the Swedish Theatre (1838) and on the north side the Orthodox church (1846) designed by Engel's department of Public Works.

Helsinki

PLATES 70–76

Senate Square is the centre of the Government area planned by Ehrenström when Helsinki was made the capital of Finland in 1812 and built by C. L. Engel. It measures about 560 ft. by 330 ft. and slopes from north to south. At the top of the slope stands the Lutheran cathedral (see Chapter 4), on a platform reached by a flight of steps. These, together with the pavilions at either end, were added in the 1840s (a few years after Engel's death), replacing a colonnaded walk for sentries. In the centre of the square is a bronze monument (1894) to the Czar Alexander II, the most liberal of the Russian czars and the most sympathetic towards Finnish aspirations.

The Senate House (now the Council of State building), occupying the whole of the east side of the square, was Engel's first large civic building in Helsinki. It was built in 1818–22. The four-storey frontage to the square, which has a central Corinthian portico embracing the two upper storeys, is returned round the corner of Aleksanterinkatu on the south to form the end pavilion of the south façade. The same form of pavilion is repeated at the other end, and between them is a two-storey wing with Ionic pilasters and, in the centre, Ionic columns and a pediment marking the south entrance. The eastern wing of this large range of buildings – a hollow square in plan – was not completed until 1826 and a northern wing was added after Engel's death.

Opposite the Senate House, on the west side of the square, is the main university building (C. L. Engel, 1828–32). It originally consisted of a square central block with staircase hall in front and semicircular auditorium behind and four-storey wings on either side, but additions were later made at the rear and the auditorium was destroyed by bombing in 1944. It was rebuilt and at the same time enlarged. The original three-storey staircase hall, with galleries supported on Doric columns, survives.

The University Library (1836–45), facing the western side of the cathedral, contains three reading-rooms, the main central one having a shallow domed roof with clerestory lighting and a gallery resting on Corinthian columns. The richly modelled ceilings and vaults had further decoration added to them by F. A. Sjöström in 1879, and an extension was built at the back (G. Nyström, architect) in 1906. Externally the building has a giant order of Corinthian pilasters with semicircular openings in the attic storey above the cornice at either end, providing clerestory lighting to the two smaller reading-rooms.

Adjoining the library on the north, in Unioninkatu, which continues the western side of Senate Square, is a group of three two-storey

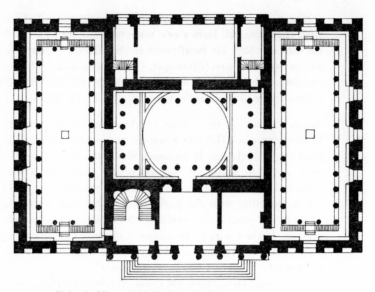

University Library, Helsinki: plan as first built

buildings by Engel, linked by low Doric gateways. These were built in 1826–32 as a Russian military hospital and are now a hospital for internal diseases.

Senate Square slopes down to the Market Square and south harbour, being separated from them first by the miscellaneous buildings forming the south side of the square (smaller in scale than the others – a survival of the pre-Engel town – and including one eighteenth-century house at the south-east corner) and secondly by the even-fronted line of buildings facing the harbour. These are shown in Plate 76. From left to right they are: the city hall (1833) by Engel; a smaller neoclassical building (1815) originally a hotel, by Pehr Granstedt; the Swedish Embassy (1922), by Torben Grut; the large building at the end, which is the Supreme Court (1883) by F. A. Sjöström. Hidden by the last is the President's Palace (1813) by Pehr Granstedt, set back behind a forecourt of which the projecting wings can just be seen. It was originally a private residence and was converted to serve as the Czar's Helsinki palace. Beyond it, set back once again and facing the neck of land that joins the Katajanokka promontory to the mainland (and therefore separates the south from the north harbour) is a single-storey neoclassical guardhouse. The distant views of this promontory are commanded by the tall brick mass and gilded turrets of the Uspenski Orthodox cathedral (A. N. Gornostajeff, 1868), seen on the right of the photograph. Since the photograph was taken, however, Alvar Aalto's Enzo-Gutzeit building (see page 86) has been built in front of it and to the right – a five-storey rectangular block designed to continue the line of pale-coloured façades shown in the photograph.

Lappeenranta
PLATE 77

This flourishing town in eastern Finland, on rising ground above Lake Saimaa, became a Russian frontier town after 1743 (see Chapter 4). In Kauppakatu, the street that connects the lake shore with the green space on which stands the town church (one of the wooden churches of Salonen, a master-builder active in east Finland, built in 1795 and with a tower added in 1856) is a modest but neatly designed town-hall – a single-storey weather-boarded building with a clock-turret as high as itself. It was built in 1829, when the town began to move from the garrison area to its present position. Until 1890 the town market occupied the space, now a garden, between the building and the street. The town-hall was the work of a surveyor called Palmroth who is known to have based his design on drawings from a volume of type designs issued from the Public Works office of which Engel had charge – an indication of the way Engel spread his architectural style and standards to the remotest corners of Finland; also of the way buildings attributed to him were often, in fact, only his designs at, as it were, several removes.

Hämeenlinna
Swedish
Tavastehus
PLATE 78

This town, the capital of Häme province, still retains in the centre some of the formal layout it was given when it moved to its present site, from one a little further north, in 1779. Its centre is a sloping market square, at the upper or eastern end of which stands the church by Desprez described in Chapter 4. On the north side, shown in the photograph, is the prefecture, a typical provincial (but none the less elegant) neo-classical building of 1833–36.

I

62.   Porvoo. Old Town Hall (1764).

70. Helsinki. Senate Square from the air. C. L. Engel (1818–40): Senate House in foreground; main university building on far side; Cathedral on right.

71. Helsinki. Senate House. C. L. Engel (1818–22): main frontage to Senate Square.

72. Helsinki. University Library. C. L. Engel (1836–45): side view with Cathedral beyond.

73. Helsinki. University Library: interior.

74. Helsinki.
Main University
Building. C. L.
Engel (1828–
1832): view across
Senate Square
from terrace
of Cathedral.

75. Helsinki.
Military Hospital
– now part
of civil hospital.
C. L. Engel
(1826–32).

76. Helsinki. Buildings facing South Harbour: city-hall (C. L. Engel, 1833) on left; Orthodox Cathedral far right.

77. Lappeenranta.
Town Hall.
Palmroth (1829).

78. Hämeenlinna.
Market Square
with Prefecture
(1833–36).

7 Wooden Town Houses

FOR THE CONNOISSEUR OF VERNACULAR STYLES OF BUILDING FINNISH towns are fascinating places, full of unrecorded treasures and unexpected variations on a common theme. They will not remain so for long because the inevitable process of modernization and rebuilding means that the streets of low wooden houses, of which all Finnish towns at one time wholly consisted, are being swept away, and it is these buildings, with their endless variety of treatment and ornament, that constitute the Finnish town vernacular.

Being built of wood, the domestic buildings – and to a great extent the commercial buildings also – were seldom more than one or two storeys high, though they were sometimes raised above the pavement on low stone basements. The combination of their consistent lowness, of their horizontal roof-lines and of the great width of the streets, produces the distinctive look of the old-style Finnish town – a look, based on the proportion of vertical to horizontal surface, which the Finnish town shares with the Russian provincial town. In spite of the absence of height it is not a suburban look, since there is no scattering of buildings with space opening out between them, no sense of streets winding away into the country. Streets are continuously built up and enclose geometrically laid out, truly urban, spaces. There is nevertheless a refreshing sense of breadth about the traditional Finnish townscape, and of the sky dominating the scene, to which the yellow ochre, white and grey of the paintwork, and the flat façades – modulated, but only lightly, by fanciful carpenter's ornament – contributes an unusual mixture of austerity and idiosyncrasy.

These broad streets, as the introductory chapter of this book observes, have the functional purpose of preventing the spread of fire. And the fire hazard is

K

one of the reasons why this town vernacular has been disappearing during recent years. Other, equally obvious, reasons are the need for multi-storey buildings, for which wood construction is unsuitable, and the general tendency to congregate in towns, and the result is that the Finnish town, which for centuries was no more than a modest trading and administrative centre at the service of a mainly rural population, has now become almost as much the typical environment of the people as it is in other European countries. In the thriving modern towns, with their substantial buildings, heavy traffic and energetic exploitation of advanced technology, the old wooden houses can no longer claim a place.

In some towns, such as Porvoo and Loviisa, where the redevelopment has taken place somewhat apart from the old centre, streets of wooden houses of some antiquity can still be seen and are likely to remain if only as a sedulously preserved historical relic, but in most towns the wooden houses that have not yet been swept away to make room for new developments are of no great age. They may belong to the latter part of last century or the early years of this, and are the work of local builders who presumably garnered ideas for their endlessly varied architectural embellishments from pattern-books and other illustrated publications.

The buildings are framed in wood and covered with boarding; sometimes vertical, sometimes horizontal. The embellishments take many forms: classical pilasters (often of eccentric proportions), window and door hoods, cornices (carved and bracketed) and fretted gables and barge-boards. They are naïve and of course quite untutored from the point of view of the correct use of the classical vocabulary from which – at several removes – they are derived. But they possess great individual charm – quite apart from the consistency they give to the urban scene when they survive in any quantity.

The examples illustrated here, following the earlier examples from the old part of Porvoo, are taken from Turku and from Tampere – both large towns from which this type of vernacular architecture will soon have disappeared altogether. It has already almost disappeared from Helsinki, and will presumably gradually disappear even from the smaller towns where it still predominates. This is an inevitable process, but this lively vernacular architecture, so wholly characteristic of the Finnish urban scene, deserves at least to be recorded before the process is complete.

Porvoo
Swedish Borgå
PLATES 79 and 80

The old part of the town – see also page 50 – retains its wooden houses, some surviving from the eighteenth century, irregularly sited along winding lanes on the medieval pattern. The second photograph from Porvoo shows wooden houses of somewhat later date, in the street which leads downhill from the old town-hall (Plate 62). They have stone basements and horizontal boarding, with naïvely applied pilasters and other carpenter's ornaments.

Turku
Swedish Åbo
PLATES 81, 82 and 84

One- and two-storey nineteenth-century wooden houses, with typical pattern-book embellishments, still survive in parts of Turku. The other photograph from Turku is taken looking into the yard between two terraces of similar houses, from which the houses are entered through double porches serving every pair.

Tampere
PLATES 83, 85 and 86

The examples chosen from Tampere show the use of both horizontal and vertical boarding and of more fanciful ornament, and include an elaborate gabled house with a plastered lower storey, exhibiting an interesting consistency of architectural treatment between it and the wooden superstructure.

79.   Porvoo. Street in the old town.

80. Porvoo. Wooden houses near the old town hall.
81. Turku. Old wooden houses.
82. Turku. Old wooden houses.
83. Tampere. Old wooden houses.
84. Turku. Wooden house-porches.

84

85

85. Tampere. Old wooden houses.
86. Tampere. Wooden house.

86

8   Styles of the Later Nineteenth Century

FROM THE DECLINE OF THE UBIQUITOUS NEOCLASSICAL IDIOM IN THE middle of the nineteenth century until national romanticism gave its new twist to architectural aspirations at the beginning of the twentieth, Finnish architects and their patrons exhibited their skill at historical reminiscence much as they did elsewhere in Europe. The feeling for classical form, however, was not lost – witness such late examples of design within the code of classical discipline as Gustaf Nyström's official buildings in Helsinki, the State Archives building (1890) and the House of Estates (1891) or, to take a provincial example, the handsome military academy at Hamina (1898). The influence of the Gothic Revival was less strongly felt, except in church architecture.

The mid-nineteenth century was not a period of great building activity; it was the time of the Crimean War, of political repression, of famines and social stagnation. But after 1862, when a more liberal political regime coincided with the building of railways and a consequent expansion of commercial activity, towns began to play a more dominant part in Finnish life and large urban buildings of many kinds – offices, stores, theatres, warehouses – were newly in demand. They began the process, which is still going on today, of replacing with substantial multi-storey structures the low wooden buildings that had hitherto occupied the centres of towns.

These new official and commercial buildings of stone, brick and plaster usually employed a renaissance idiom of a kind. It was sometimes fairly ornate, but even so the flatness of surface and the overall simplicity of geometrical form which are common to all the preceding eras of Finnish architecture were generally maintained. At this time also Finland embarked on the gradual process

L

of industrialization, its start being marked by an ambitious industrial exhibition – the equivalent of those so successfully held in London, Paris and elsewhere – at Helsinki in 1876. Significantly, though, the specially constructed exhibition hall was wholly of wood.

Up till Engel's death, the office of the Controller of Public Works, of which he was in charge for sixteen years, served as the principal nursery of young architects. Afterwards the leading architects were mostly Stockholm-trained: for example Chiewitz, whose work I have already referred to (page 42), and Carl Theodor Höijer, the outstanding architect of large commercial buildings in the 1880s and the architect also of the National Gallery of Art (*Ateneum*), 1887. Finland acquired its own architectural school when the Polytechnic Institute was set up in Helsinki in 1872.

After the end of the century Finnish architecture was dominated by the, in many ways unique, National Romantic movement which is the subject of the next chapter. This and the Arts and Crafts and *Art Nouveau* influences associated with it opened the door to modern architecture, which is dealt with in its experimental phases in the chapter after and in its post-war maturity in the last chapter of all. But the eclectic styles continued to have a place in Finnish architecture until at least the 1930s, as they did in that of other countries during the years when modern architectural principles were gradually asserting themselves. In Finland they were thrown even further into the background by the completeness with which national romanticism dominated the scene in the early years of the century. The continued employment of reminiscent or historical styles during the twentieth century can appropriately be recorded in this chapter because it perpetuated a mode of architectural thinking characteristic of the nineteenth century, and it can be adequately represented by a couple of instances: the theatre at Tampere and the Parliament building at Helsinki (1927–31), the most prominent example of that tasteful but often somewhat emasculated classicism with which Sweden imbued the world of architectural fashion for a whole generation between the wars.

Loviisa
PLATE 87

The town-hall, occupying the centre of one side of the long, tree-planted market square, is a transitional building, preserving the simple geometrical form of the neoclassical period but incorporating eclectically chosen details, some with a Gothic flavour, and surmounted by a picturesque Italianate tower. It was designed in 1856 by Georg Theodor Chiewitz, one of the leading architects of the middle of the century – see also his church at Pori, Plate 56.

Loviisa is an agreeable town and summer resort at the head of a gulf, the entrance to which was once guarded by the marine fortress of

Svartholm. It was founded in 1745, with the name of Degerby, as a fortified outpost on the eastern border of Swedish-controlled territory, and renamed in 1752 after the wife of the Swedish King Adolph-Frederik, who visited it in that year. The fortifications, after being surrendered to the Russians in 1808, were destroyed by the British during the Crimean War. Besides the town-hall Loviisa contains a number of buildings of interest: the late seventeenth-century manor-house of Degerby (now a tourist centre), some narrow streets of eighteenth-century wooden houses, the municipal museum, built in 1755 as a residence for the commandant of the fortress, and a neo-gothic church of 1865, also by Chiewitz. Near by on the road to Kotka, at Ruotsin-pyhtää, are the eighteenth-century wooden buildings of a waterside ironworks, one of Finland's earliest examples of industrial building.

Helsinki
PLATES 88–90

The House of the Nobility (1861), Plate 88, is another and more ambitious design by Chiewitz in brick and stone, but again introducing traceried windows and other Gothic-flavoured details into a flat symmetrical façade subdivided vertically and horizontally in renaissance fashion. It stands north-east of the Lutheran cathedral and contains an impressive stairway and a large assembly hall with beamed ceiling and panelled walls adorned with armorial bearings.

The office building shown in Plate 89 is in Erottaja, Helsinki, and is one of the best examples of the richly detailed neo-renaissance town buildings of the 1880s. It is by Carl Theodor Höijer, the leading architect of his time, and was built in 1889. Höijer was trained in Sweden and then became a pupil of Chiewitz in the latter's office at Turku. The building is now occupied by the Government Forestry Board.

The House of Estates (1891), Plate 90, is a typical example of the work of Gustaf Nyström and shows how, in his hands, the neoclassical tradition was continued up to the end of the century with considerable vigour and assurance. The pediment above the Corinthian portico has bronze sculpture by E. Wikström (1903). The building stands to the north-east of Senate Square, in Snellmaninkatu. In it, and its predecessor, the national diet (consisting of four estates – the nobility, the clergy, the burgesses and the peasants) met from 1863, when the liberal Czar Alexander II summoned it for the first time since 1809, until 1906 when single-chamber government was instituted. The building now houses various scientific societies.

Hamina
Swedish
Fredrikshamn
PLATE 91

The main building of the military academy (school for reserve officers) is another example of the continuation right up to the end of the century – the building is dated 1898 – of the traditions and disciplines of the neoclassical era. The academy was built during the Russian regime for the training of Finnish cadets. The remarkably planned eighteenth-century fortress town of Hamina is described on pages 19 and 51 and shown from the air in Plate 63.

Tampere

PLATE 92

The municipal theatre (1912) is a late neoclassical building by Kauno S. Kallio, Greek in flavour but showing also something of the *Art Nouveau* phase through which Finnish architecture had just been passing. It maintains at the same time the flatness of façade modelling that is characteristic of Finnish architecture of whatever era. The theatre stands on the eastern side of the central square of Tampere, near one of the bridges across the rapids (linking two lakes at different levels) round which the town is built and from which it originally (1820 onwards) derived its industrial importance. In the same square as the theatre is the Old Church (Bassi, 1824; bell-tower by Engel). Tampere's most distinguished building is the cathedral by Lars Sonck, described in the next chapter.

Helsinki

PLATE 93

The Parliament building at Helsinki (1927–31) is Finland's most prominent example of the formalized neoclassical style that was developed in Sweden in the 1920s (e.g. Ivar Tengbom's Stockholm concert-hall) and much imitated elsewhere. It is a monumental composition of red granite, which loses some of its effect by standing in bleak isolation beside the Mannerheimintie, one of Helsinki's main arteries, without being tied into its surroundings by supporting buildings or sympathetic landscaping. The architect was J. S. Sirén, the winner (with his then partners Borg and Åberg) of a competition held in 1924. It has a symmetrical plan with a high circular hall in the centre.

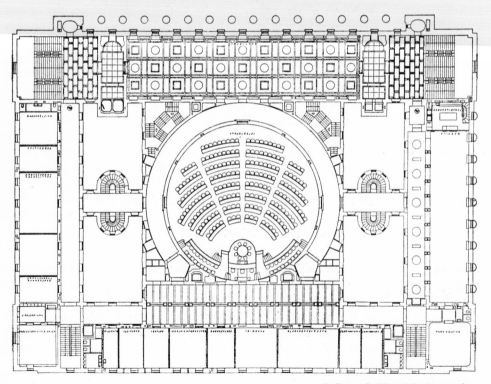

Parliament Building, Helsinki: main floor

87. Loviisa. Town Hall. G. T. Chiewitz (1856).
88. Helsinki. House of the Nobility. G. T. Chiewitz (1861).

89. Helsinki. Office building in Erottaja. C. T. Hoijer (1869).
90. Helsinki. House of Estates. Gustaf Nyström (1891).
91. Hamina. Military Academy (1898).

92. Tampere. Municipal Theatre.
K. S. Kallio (1912).
93. Helsinki. Parliament Building.
J. S. Sirén (1927–31).

93

9   National Romanticism and Art Nouveau

IN MOST EUROPEAN COUNTRIES THE LATER YEARS OF THE NINETEENTH century saw efforts on the part of pioneer architects and designers to find ways of escape from the academic strait-jacket and the cultural meaninglessness of applied historical styles. These efforts took various forms: in England, through the Arts and Crafts movement founded by William Morris, they placed a new emphasis on truth to materials, especially as practised by the medieval crafts-man; on the continent of Europe, through the *Art Nouveau* movement initiated in Belgium by Victor Horta and Henri van de Velde, they fostered the develop-ment of a consciously non-historical style of design and ornamentation, linear in character and influenced by new developments in art and a newly awakened interest in the Orient.

In Finland, equivalent efforts began with the revival of peasant styles of building, especially those of Karelia. This revival, though inspired by the same impulses as inspired Morris and his associates in England, was also a product of the political situation in Finland and the feelings engendered by it. A deeply felt need for a sense of national identity, fortified by the repressions of the Russian regime, which at that time was increasingly denying Finland the autonomy the country had theoretically possessed since 1809, and the use even of its native language, found expression in representations and reminders of Finland's roots in the past, and among these were Finland's local architectural traditions. The same urge towards a national identity found expression in the music of Sibelius and the paintings of Axel Gallén-Kallela. In 1894 the latter built himself a studio at Ruovesi using the methods of the Karelian log-house, and in the same year Lars Sonck (1870–1956), then a newly qualified architect of only 24, built a villa of logs on the Åland Islands.

M

Sonck was one of a group of architects who, as students at the Helsinki Polytechnic Institute, had developed this urge towards architectural emancipation and this romantic feeling for Finnish vernacular traditions. Others of the group were Eliel Saarinen (1873–1950), Armas Lindgren and Herman Gesellius. These last three, in 1896, went into partnership together and in due course made plans to build for themselves a range of studios and dwellings where they could work and live together in a secluded and congenial atmosphere of their own creation. They found a site at Hvitträsk, on the edge of a lake to the west of Helsinki. They were able to embark on this ambitious project because, in 1899, they had won first prize in the competition for the design of the Finnish pavilion at the Paris exhibition of 1900 – a success which gave them the beginnings of a practice. Their Paris design itself reflected their generation's interest in Finland's early vernacular architecture. Inside, the pavilion had mural paintings by Gallén-Kallela.

The first buildings to be completed at Hvitträsk were strongly influenced by the farmhouse architecture of Karelia, but as the project developed it became more sophisticated and less directly derived from primitive models. Especially evident was the influence of the English domestic architecture that had sprung from the Arts and Crafts movement – the work of Norman Shaw, Voysey and Philip Webb and, most notably, of Baillie Scott. Their houses would have become familiar to the younger Finnish architects through the pages of *The Studio*, which had started publication in 1893 and had a wide European circulation.

There was also a closer connection with English trends and ideas in the person of A. W. Finch, an English artist who had lived in Belgium (where he had collaborated with van de Velde), and who taught for many years at the Helsinki school of craft and design, of which Armas Lindgren was made director in 1902. Along with the architects named above, Finch was a member of a group of like-minded artists, architects and writers from whose work and proselytizing activities this new approach to architecture emerged. Among Finch's contributions to the group's magazine *Ateneum* was an article about the English Arts and Crafts movement. Another influential writer was Gustaf Strengell, author of a number of far-sighted books on art and design – his writings are in many ways comparable with those of W. R. Lethaby in England – and another architect who had direct contact with the new ideas emerging, and the experiments taking place, elsewhere in Europe was Sigurd Frosterus, who also worked with van de Velde and expounded his ideas in writing in Finland.

Van de Velde's pioneer work embraced of course a new functional approach to architectural design, which was later to be reflected in the work of several Finnish architects, as well as a new non-historical style of decoration. The influence of the latter can clearly be seen in Finland in some of the furnishings of Hvitträsk – Saarinen, Lindgren and Gesellius would have been made thoroughly familiar with it at the 1900 Paris exhibition; van de Velde's *Art*

Nouveau interiors and furniture had indeed been seen in Paris as early as 1896.

The same trio of architects designed a number of other domestic buildings, including blocks of flats notable for their picturesque sculptural massing, in this new National Romantic style, and (in 1902) a country house at Suur-Merijoki, near Viipuri – now demolished – with interiors and furnishings resembling those of C. F. A. Voysey. These were followed by the Pohjola Insurance Company's offices in Aleksanterinkatu, Helsinki (1901), a bank building in Helsinki (1904 – demolished 1934) and – the building that first brought the new style prominently before the public eye, and was at the same time the most extravagantly romantic and nostalgic of them all – the National Museum at Helsinki. They won the competition for this in 1902 although actual building was not started until 1905. During the same opening years of the century, the other outstanding exponent of the National Romantic style, Lars Sonck, built a number of important works: a church in Turku (1905), the cathedral at Tampere (1902–07) and the telephone building at Helsinki (1905).

Characteristic of all these buildings was their rugged granite stonework – even more rugged than that favoured by another pioneer, the American H. H. Richardson, by whom, in addition to the European pioneers, the young Finnish architects may have been to some extent influenced – their spiky silhouettes crowning a free picturesque grouping of masses, and their reminiscences of motifs found in Finnish medieval churches and fortresses. External ornament, concentrated for the most part round door and window openings, took the form of stone carving more closely resembling the free inventions of Louis Sullivan than directly imitating antique models. Their interiors were notable for their efforts to combine the work of craftsmen and painters into a unified whole – a whole with usually a marked *Art Nouveau* or Arts and Crafts flavour. Other examples of the National Romantic style that deserve mention are the National Theatre, Helsinki, near the railway station (Onni Tarjanne, 1902), and the students' union of the Polytechnic Institute (Walter Thomé and Karl Lindahl, 1903).

The most wilfully picturesque and nostalgic phase of National Romanticism gave way before long to a style of design more international than national – more closely related, that is, to the new approach to design evolving on the continent of Europe. The work being done in Europe – whether called *Art Nouveau* in Brussels and Paris or *Jugendstil* in central Europe, whether pioneered by van de Velde or the English group of small house designers or the Scottish Mackintosh or the Viennese Hoffmann – had, as we have seen, been part of the inspiration of the younger Finnish architects since the late 1890s, though their participation in a Europe-wide movement of emancipation had been disguised, as it were, by the local colouring that National Romanticism had given it.

Perhaps the first sign of the transition from romanticism to rationalism was a small hospital designed by Lars Sonck in 1905 in the Helsinki suburb of Eira, with plain white walls and little embellishment, but the most significant change came with the design of the railway station at Helsinki. This again was the subject of a competition, held in 1904 and again won by Saarinen, Lindgren and Gesellius. Their first design retained some of the romantic characteristics with which this trio had made its name, but before being built (1906–14) it was revised by Saarinen alone and given a simpler and more regular form, more directly reflecting its means of construction. Though the building is richly embellished, ornament takes second place to enclosure of space and expressiveness of structure.

Saarinen was thus moving more in the direction of European rationalism, a development no doubt accelerated by a number of tours he made in these years, accompanied by his wife – the sister of Gesellius – whom he had married in 1904. In that year they travelled through Germany, England and Scotland, and in 1907 they toured Germany again and – very significantly – visited Josef Olbrich in Darmstadt and Peter Behrens in Berlin. From these years dates Saarinen's interest in urban design which was to play an important part in his subsequent career. In 1907, too, he won first prize in a competition for a Finnish Parliament House, with a symmetrical building with a central tower – plain but somewhat heavily monumental – which was never built for political reasons.

The later work of Lars Sonck became, like Saarinen's, more formal and less dependent on the freedom of the picturesque ; witness his symmetrically composed bank building of 1908 in the Esplanade at Helsinki, his church in the Helsinki suburb of Kallio (1909–12) and his Helsinki stock exchange (1911). These, though still highly personal in style, are duller than his early buildings, having discarded that slight element of the grotesque which gave the latter their idiosyncratic character without acquiring, like the best of Saarinen's, the different kind of vigour derived from new building techniques.

A number of commercial buildings designed around this time, by Lindgren, Frosterus, Selim Lindqvist (an architect of a slightly older generation whose work had always been coloured by international rather than national influences and who was the first to build, in 1906, with a steel frame), Jarl Eklund and others, helped to establish a respectable idiom for city buildings that combined a functional sobriety of form with a sparing but inventive use of ornament.

One of the most interesting phenomena of these years was the residential suburb of Eira in the southern part of Helsinki. Laid out in 1907 with winding roads in approved Garden City style, lined with individually designed informal white-walled villas, it possesses unusual consistency. The villas, many of which are the work of Selim Lindqvist, again show the influence of contemporary English domestic architecture.

In other countries than Finland the work of the small minority of architects designing in this, in the *Art Nouveau* and in the other emancipated styles, though of great significance as the forerunners of profounder changes, was but a small part of the totality of buildings. It did no more than give occasional piquancy to a scene still – in the first two decades of the twentieth century – dominated by applied historical styles and the impulsive search for picturesque effect. But in Finland it represented a large part of the country's building effort and, in Helsinki particularly, dominated the architectural scene – a unique situation, attributable to the widespread support given, especially by their fellow intellectuals, to the pioneer efforts of the young romanticists, to the absence of any deeply entrenched public opinion to act as a brake on the acceptance of unfamiliar ideas, to the regular use of the competition system which threw open the greatest opportunities to the emerging talent and to the simple circumstance that the men who became, during these years, the leading architects in the country were also the most thoughtful, open-minded and adventurous.

The result was not only to make Finland a country of unusual interest today to students of the new architectural movements of the opening years of this century but, by relieving Finnish architecture of the oppressive burden of preconceived styles and attitudes which the modern movement had to struggle so persistently to shake off, to prepare the ground more thoroughly than in most other places for the eventual acceptance of the new architecture described in the next two chapters.

Hvitträsk
PLATES 94 and 95

The studio-office and group of dwellings designed from 1901 onwards for their joint use by Eliel Saarinen, Armas Lindgren and Herman Gesellius, on a wooded site rising steeply from the edge of a lake about 15 miles west of Helsinki. The first part to be built (1902), which the three young architects occupied temporarily while work on the remainder was going forward, consisted of a studio and workshop (later to be used as stables) with a large flat above (later to be Gesellius's dwelling). It was simple in style, reminiscent of Karelian vernacular building, but the remainder of the project is more original and sophisticated in style and shows the influence of the new domestic architecture (itself based,

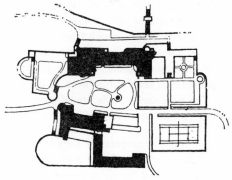

Hvitträsk: layout plan

of course, on a revived interest in vernacular building methods) that had lately emerged in Europe and particularly in England. It consists of a long range of buildings, characteristically irregular in outline, with the single-storey studio in the centre and a two-storey L-shaped dwelling at either end, enclosing, with the first building, a rectangular courtyard. Materials were stone, partly plastered over, shingles and pantiles for the roofs.

The dwelling at the entrance end, occupied by Lindgren, had originally a square timber-faced tower surmounted by a tile-covered turret, but it was badly damaged in a fire and subsequently rebuilt to a smaller size and without the tower. The other dwelling, which has an additional storey in the roof, was occupied by Saarinen. On its far side the ground falls away steeply, and here the romantic siting of the buildings becomes evident. Overlooking the woods and the lake beyond, they are surrounded by terraces and loggias and half a century's growth of vegetation. These garden outworks are additions made over the years by Saarinen, for in the course of time Hvitträsk became solely his. Lindgren left the partnership in 1905 and Gesellius in 1907. Saarinen made alterations to adapt the whole complex of buildings to his taste and lived and worked there until he emigrated to America in 1923.

The interiors preserve much of his idiosyncratic, inventive Arts and Crafts detail, including vast tile-faced fireplaces embellished with copper and iron and furniture influenced by van de Velde, and there was a nursery resembling some of C. R. Mackintosh's interiors in Glasgow. The treatment of space and the subtle use of changes of level remarkably anticipate Frank Lloyd Wright's work as a pioneer of the open plan, although Saarinen cannot have known of this at the time Hvitträsk was designed. Hvitträsk is now in private hands, the present owners having acquired it half derelict in 1949 and meticulously restored it. The only substantial change they made was to open up the main living-room of the original Saarinen dwelling into the studio-office which was previously entered only from the courtyard.

Helsinki
PLATE 96

The National Museum, by Saarinen, Lindgren and Gesellius (designed 1901; built 1905–12) was the outcome of a competition and was these three architects' first major building in the National Romantic style which they, together with Lars Sonck, were chiefly responsible for developing. Note in this early effort, as well as the picturesque irregularity of the composition, the not fully assimilated elements from Finnish medieval architecture such as the geometrical ornament in the gable. The rock-faced walls are of granite, the carved stonework of sandstone and the spire of brick roofed with copper.

Tampere
PLATES 97–100

The Cathedral at Tampere by Lars Sonck was the subject of a competition held in 1899 and was built 1902–07. It is Sonck's most successful building and his most important contribution to the National Romantic style, with its historical reminiscences well assimilated into a

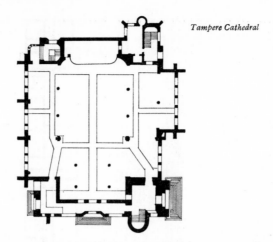

Tampere Cathedral

bold and irregular but coherent composition. It has a square plan with a wide star-vaulted nave, narrow galleried aisles (widened on the south side to form a shallow transept) and the shallowest possible sanctuary, creating a spatial effect similar to that of the earlier Finnish cruciform churches in spite of its marked west-east axis. The latter is disguised externally by the typically romantic difference in size between the two western towers. Except around the west door, there is no embellishment outside but the pronounced textures of the materials – coursed rock-faced granite and red tiles. Inside, the style is orthodox *Art Nouveau*. The wall-paintings are by Hugo Simberg except for the Resurrection over the altar, which is by Magnus Enckell.

Helsinki
PLATE 101

The Telephone Building (1905) in Korkeavuorenkatu, by Lars Sonck, is typical of his romantic phase. The skilfully balanced façade (in spite of every group of windows being a different shape) is all in granite – rock-faced but relieved by the smooth door-surround and horizontal bands. In accordance with Finnish historical traditions there is only the minimum of ornament, in the form of incised geometrical designs round the columns.

Imatra
PLATES 102 and 103

The picturesque Valtion (National) Hotel was built in 1903 alongside the rapids formed by the Vuoksi river cutting its way through the steep rocky landscape to give the waters of Lake Saimaa – Finland's largest lake – an outlet into Lake Ladoga. The rapids, which now lie almost on the Russian frontier, were a popular place of resort until a large power station was built (1921–29) across the river from the hotel, lessening both the force of the water and the charm of the scenery. The hotel, though much altered within, is an excellent early example of Finnish *Art Nouveau*, with picturesque elements that link it also to the National Romantic movement. It was the principal work of its architect, Usko Nyström, who later became even more original and independent and was a teacher with unusually advanced ideas.

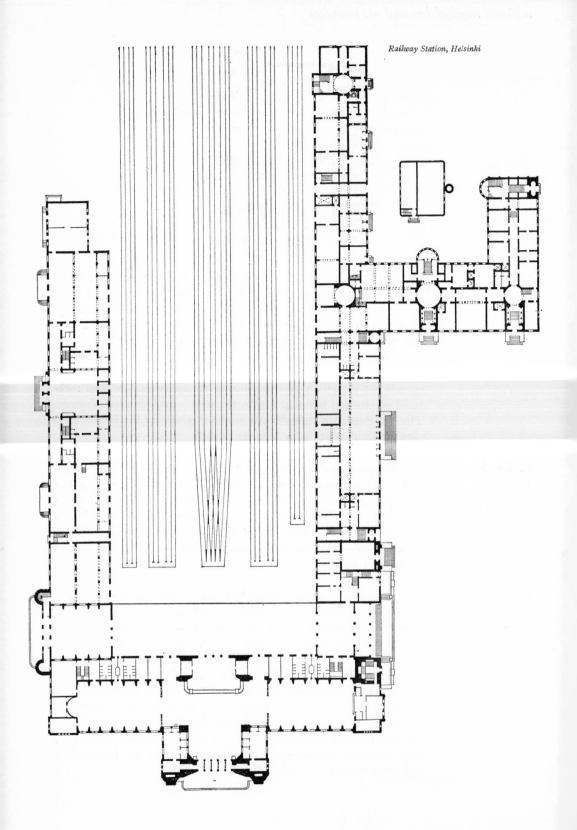

Railway Station, Helsinki

The Railway Station, Plates 104 and 105, was the subject of a competition held in 1904 and won by Saarinen, Lindgren and Gesellius. It was built to Saarinen's revised design in 1906–14. It is a key building, since it provides the link between these architects' first romantic phase and the later, more rational, phase in which the modernity of their ideas is no longer overlaid by archaic affectations and picturesquely used references to Finnish architectural history. In the plan, which is symmetrical except for the clock-tower at the south-east corner and an administrative wing to the north-east, the main elements are the central hall, with the main entrance under the great arch which forms one end, and two secondary halls at right-angles. All three have vaulted roofs in reinforced concrete (used here for the first time in a major public building in Finland), and these halls are clearly expressed in the external massing; the whole building in fact, in spite of some wilful stylizations, is a well-articulated reflection of the internal spaces and the structural means of enclosing them. The walls are granite and the roofs copper. The pairs of giant sculptured figures flanking the main entrance are by Emil Wikström.

The Mortgage bank building in the Esplanade (1908), Plate 106, and the church at Kallio, a northern district of Helsinki (1909–12), Plate 107, are both by Lars Sonck, and are typical of his work at this time when he had replaced romantic picturesqueness by more formalized compositions, incorporating classical elements. His skill in juxtaposing masonry textures and in the placing of ornament is still there, but the result is somewhat stiff and lacking in vitality. The Kallio church was the subject of a competition held in 1906.

Eira, Plates 108 and 109, is a compact residential area in the southernmost part of Helsinki, separated from the waterfront only by a main road and railway. It was laid out on Garden City principles, with winding roads designed to be lined with individual villas, in 1907, by Bertel Jung, Lindgren and Sonck, and was completely built up within a few years afterwards so that it presented – and still presents – a very consistent picture of the sophisticated taste in small house architecture of this time. The influence of English architects like Voysey and Baillie Scott can be clearly discerned, though the smooth white walls and simple geometrical forms have little in common with the nostalgic rusticity of materials and textures associated with much of these architects' work. Even more evident in the Eira villas is the influence of the Viennese *Jugend* style. Selim Lindqvist, who designed many of them, employed this style with assurance and sensibility. The flats shown in Plate 108 were built in 1911 and have now been demolished.

Tampere

PLATE 110

An *Art Nouveau* influenced building with great charm of detail is the fire station at Tampere, designed in 1907 by Vivi Lönn, who was one of the first women to practise architecture in Finland. She specialized in schools and worked for a time in partnership with Lindgren. She was born in 1872 and at the time of writing (1966) is still alive.

N

Lahti

PLATE III

This thriving modern industrial town (Finland's fourth largest) has a town-hall by Eliel Saarinen, built in 1912 following a competition held the previous year. It is typical of his late manner: restrained, precise, almost classical in feeling and relying largely on subtle changes of material and texture. Only the sparsely displayed ornament provides any reminder of the architect's *Art Nouveau* and other revolutionary allegiances.

Hvitträsk.
[Saa]rinen,
[Lin]dgren and
[Ge]sellius (1902):
[Eli]el Saarinen's
[hou]se from
entrance
[cou]rtyard.

Hvitträsk:
[the] garden side.

96.   Helsinki. National Museum. Saarinen,
Lindgren and Gesellius (1901).
97.   Tampere Cathedral. Lars Sonck (1902–
1907): the west end.
98.   Tampere Cathedral: entrance gateway.

99.   Tampere Cathedral. Lars Sonck (1902–07): west door and base of tower.
100. Tampere Cathedral: interior.
101. Helsinki. Telephone Building. Lars Sonck (1905).

102.   Imatra. Valtion Hotel. Usko Nyström (1903).

103. Imatra. Valtion Hotel.

104. Helsinki. Railway Station. Eliel Saarinen (1906–14).
105. Helsinki. Railway Station: main entrance.

106. Helsinki. Bank building in Esplanade. Lars Sonck (1908).

107. Helsinki. Kallio Church. Lars Sonck (1909–12).

108. Helsinki. Flats at Eira. Selim Lindqvist (1911).

109. Helsinki. Houses at Eira (*c.* 1909–12).

110. Tampere.
Fire Station.
Vivi Lönn (1907).

111. Lahti. Town
Hall. Eliel Saarinen
(1912).

10 The Beginnings of Modernism: 1928–1940

AFTER 1917 FINLAND WAS AN INDEPENDENT NATION AND HAD NO MORE need to make its architecture a symbol of its urge towards a national identity – cultural or linguistic. The National Romantic phase described in the preceding chapter had in any case been largely superseded, by the time the first World War began, by simpler and more rational styles of design better suited to the needs of a modern urban civilization and reflecting the changes in aesthetic ideals then occurring in many parts of Europe. These included, as we have seen, changes arising from the revolution in domestic architecture that had taken place in England, from the *Art Nouveau* movement as it had developed in Brussels, Paris and Vienna and from parallel developments in Germany.

At the same time the philosophy that united the separate architectural experiments being conducted in different parts of Europe and America, which were eventually to lead on to the international phase of modern architecture, was being more widely understood in Finland; the writings, that is to say, of Strengell and the rationalist ideas that Frosterus had brought back from his association with van de Velde were proving to be a more lasting influence than the novelties of style that had provided the first visible evidence of change; so that the developments dealt with in the preceding chapter not only served the purpose of emancipating Finnish architecture from the academic sterility that would have stood in the way of the prompt adoption of modern architecture, but they laid the foundations of modern architecture itself. Two new factors that appeared during the years after the first World War, to encourage the building of a substantial structure on to these still somewhat tentative foundations, were a new sense of architecture's social responsibilities – resulting from the housing

o

and similar problems Finland was faced with at the end of the war – and an increasing awareness of the implications of new building techniques.

At first, however, the architecture resulting from these more rational attitudes was relatively unexciting, and some of the best of it still harked back to the earlier romanticism; for example, the Käpylä housing in Helsinki (1920–25: architect, Martti Välikangas), a charming complex of low wooden dwellings laid out in English garden-suburb style. In general, the Finnish architecture of the 1920s, though plain, had the plainness of the neoclassical tradition rather than that of the structurally more expressive functionalism that was already a powerful movement on the continent of Europe.

This movement took hold of Finland at the end of the 1920s, partly under the influence of the Swedish architect Gunnar Asplund, himself previously a neo-classicist, who signalled his conversion to functionalism at the epoch-making Stockholm exhibition of 1930, but more particularly as a result of the clear-sightedness and the example of two Finnish architects, who were both working in Turku and who had become familiar by direct experience with the new ideas current in Europe. They were Erik Bryggman (1891–1955) and Alvar Aalto (born 1898). Together they made the designs for an exhibition held in Turku in 1929 to celebrate the seven-hundredth anniversary of that town's foundation. In it, though the exhibition was a modest one, their new architectural allegiances were clearly made evident. Aalto (who had been, incidentally, a pupil of Frosterus) had already, in 1927, designed the *Turun Sanomat* newspaper building in Turku (built 1928–29) and won the competition for a public library at Viipuri (built 1930–35) – both designs being structurally advanced and uncompromisingly modern – and in 1928 he had won the competition for a building of even greater impact: the tuberculosis sanatorium at Paimio (built 1929–33), with a design showing remarkable plastic imagination as well as organic planning and structural invention. This and the Viipuri library (now in Russian territory and reconstructed after severe war damage) were Finland's first major contributions to the new international style of modern architecture.

In these buildings also Aalto first experimented with the bent plywood furniture that was later to be so closely associated with his name and was profoundly to influence furniture design all over the world. In several of their interiors, too, were foretastes of the very personal idiom he was to develop later: for example, the undulating wood-strip ceilings at Viipuri.

An architect who showed promise, before his early death, of becoming a third pioneer was Pauli Blomstedt (1900–35). He designed the Finnish Savings Bank in Helsinki (1939), a hotel at Rovaniemi (1936), a church at Kannonkoski (1938) and the very distinguished Aulanko Hotel (also 1938) in a park two and a half miles north of Hämeenlinna. The church and the Aulanko Hotel were completed after his death by Märta Blomstedt, in the case of the latter in collaboration with Matti Lampén.

Besides his most admired building, the cemetery chapel at Turku (1939),

Erik Bryggman, who stayed on in Turku after Aalto had moved to Helsinki, designed a number of other buildings there, including a hotel (1929) in a part of the town for which he also made the plan, a library (1936) for the Åbo *Akademi* – the Swedish-language university – and an insurance company's offices (1938). Other architects who designed noteworthy modern buildings in Finland during the same years were Hilding Ekelund (church at Töölö, Helsinki, 1929), Flodin and Seppälä (Tampere railway station, 1936), J. S. Sirén (the severe, plainly fenestrated office building of Lassila Tikanoja, Helsinki, of 1935, which came surprisingly soon after his highly eclectic Parliament House – see page 64), Lindegren and Jäntti (Olympic stadium, Helsinki, 1934) and Erkki Huttunen (church at Nakkila, 1937; industrial buildings at Oulu, 1938). Huttunen also made a number of designs for small wooden houses using standardized parts that interestingly anticipated the prefabricated house designs of twenty years after.

The work of these architects was sober, sincere and unassuming. The power and originality came from Alvar Aalto, who took the lead in the struggle to win acceptance in Finland for the principles of modern architecture that Gropius, Le Corbusier and the other participants in the *Congrès Internationaux d'Architecture Moderne* were spreading throughout Europe – congresses in which Aalto took an active part. In the 1930s it was his increasing authority that gave Finland its reputation as a country that had not only accepted the precepts and practices of modern architecture but was capable of making its own contribution to the process of bringing it to maturity. This was dramatically demonstrated abroad by his two Finnish pavilions – for the Paris exhibition of 1937 and the New York world fair of 1939. Though outside the scope of this book, these pavilions are too significant to ignore if only because they illustrate yet again the close connection that has always existed between the evolution of Finnish architecture and Finland's urge to establish a national identity.

In these years Alvar Aalto, as a hero figure, stood virtually alone. Lars Sonck was no longer very active, nor had his work grown away – as Saarinen's had – from his earlier romantic allegiances; and Saarinen himself, whose main enterprise after 1917 had been to prepare designs – never executed – for a monumental museum of Finnish folklore, commemorating the country's independence and set in a characteristic landscape of lakes and forests, had emigrated to America in 1923.

Helsinki

PLATE 112

The Stockmann department store in the middle of Helsinki, by Sigurd Frosterus, was the outcome of a competition held in 1916, but only a small part of it was built then, the remainder being completed between 1924 and 1930. It clearly shows, in the logical expression of its frame

77

construction, its affinity with the more advanced of the Dutch, German and other European work of the time, exemplifying principles that Frosterus had consistently followed while others of the pioneer generation of Finnish architects were liberating themselves from nineteenth-century academicism by the more roundabout route of nostalgic romanticism and formalism of various kinds.

The building is of red brick externally with a copper roof. Inside there is a column-free central hall rising the full height of the building and top lit, which the upper floors overlook in the form of galleries.

Turku
Swedish Åbo
PLATE 113

The building, in one of Turku's main streets, for the *Turun Sanomat* newspaper, was one of Aalto's first substantial commissions (built 1928–29). In it he showed his appreciation of the aesthetic potentialities of new methods of construction. The machine hall housing the printing presses and the paper storage shed have their ceilings supported by tapering and mushroom-headed reinforced concrete columns respectively, the former especially – vigorous as tree-trunks – showing great subtlety of modelling. One of Aalto's favourite devices, the cylindrical rooflight, also makes its first appearance in this building.

Paimio
PLATES 114 and 115

Alvar Aalto's tuberculosis sanatorium, remotely situated in thick forest about 18 miles east of Turku, is the building that first put Finland on the modern architectural map. Aalto's winning competition design was made in 1928 and the sanatorium was built in 1929–33. It is informally

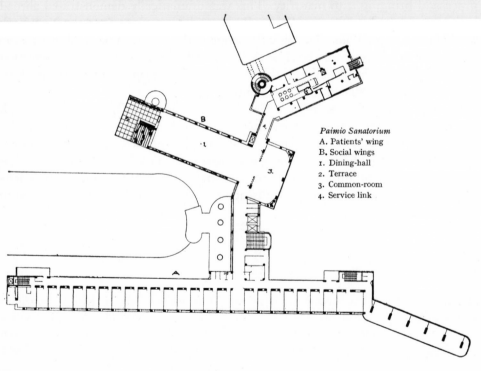

Paimio Sanatorium
A. Patients' wing
B. Social wings
1. Dining-hall
2. Terrace
3. Common-room
4. Service link

planned, each department occupying a separate wing and the wings radiating from the centre at different angles, determined by the direction of sunlight and view. The reinforced concrete frame construction is fully exposed and fully exploited aesthetically: taut and muscular, yet gracefully modulated. In Plate 115, which is taken looking east into the three-sided entrance court, the patients' wing is on the right, rising above the tree tops and turning its wide windows and balconies (which are on the far side) towards the low northern sun. The administration is in the centre and the dining and recreation rooms on the left.

Sunila
PLATES 116–118

On the coast of the Gulf of Finland, near the industrial and timber exporting town of Kotka, is the large cellulose (wood-pulp) factory of Sunila, designed together with an employees' housing estate by Alvar Aalto (1936–39) and later extended by him (1951–54). It is on the steep edge of an arm of the sea, so that sea-going ships can berth close in. The uneven rock-strewn site, instead of being blasted flat, has been dramatically exploited to allow the successive industrial processes to take place on descending levels, finishing at the quayside. A conveyor (on the left in Plate 116) takes the raw timber – a whole year's supply of logs, floated down by water or brought through the lakes by ship – to the highest point where the production sequence begins. Production buildings are brick, service and warehouse buildings white concrete.

The Sunila housing estate, Plates 117 and 118, which accommodates a thousand people, is sited inland from the factory and consists of parallel blocks of dwellings along the southern slopes of an undulating rocky site, with forest occupying the northern slopes and the access roads in the valleys between. In most of the blocks the upper floors are set back, providing open terraces in front of their windows. The steep slope allows the middle storey to be entered at ground level from the

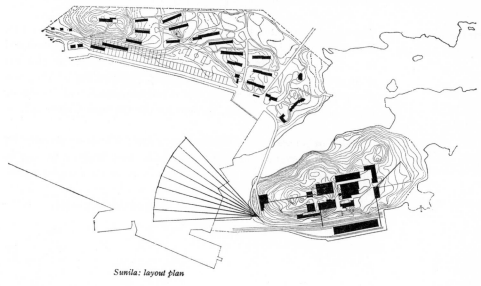

Sunila: layout plan

P

rear. At the eastern end of the site are separate houses for senior employees, standing in their own gardens. Sunila was the first important example of the patronage of modern architecture by Finnish industry; until then nearly all the modern architects' opportunities had been gained by winning competitions.

Noormarkku

PLATE 119

This country house, the Villa Mairea (by Alvar Aalto and his wife Aino Aalto, 1938–39), occupies a hilltop site in the forested landscape of western Finland, near the small village of Noormarkku, not far from Pori. The house is L-shaped, with an extension in the form of a terrace backed by a stone wall partly enclosing, with the house, a garden court. A large part of the ground floor consists of one space which can be sub-divided by movable partitions. This part of the house has a steel frame. Walls are brick, plastered. In the various wood finishes Aalto experimented here with many of the techniques he was to develop in his later work: wood strips on walls and ceilings, close-set wooden rods serving as screens and so on. He had made similar experiments, though on a less ambitious scale, in his own house in the Helsinki suburb of Munk-kiniemi, designed the year before.

Nakkila

PLATE 120

One of the first modern churches in Finland was this country church by Erkki Huttunen, built in 1937. It has a rectangular nave, seating one thousand, a side-lit sanctuary with a semicircular apse, a west tower and a crypt. The nave has a corrugated ceiling of wood boarding.

Turku

Swedish Åbo

PLATE 121

The Resurrection Chapel in the new cemetery on the south-eastern outskirts of the town is Erik Bryggman's most notable work, designed in 1939. It has a concrete frame and brick walls and an asymmetrical plan, with an aisle along only one side of the nave. The side wall, within the aisle, is wholly of glass, giving a view into foliage and trees.

Helsinki

PLATES 122–123

The Olympic stadium (by Yrjö Lindegren and Toivo Jäntti), Plate 122, is in a park at the northern end of Mannerheimintie. It was designed in 1934 for the Olympic Games planned to take place at Helsinki in 1940 but postponed because of the war. Work on the building was interrupted for the same reason, but it was completed, with its seating capacity increased to 70,000, in time for the Olympic Games held in 1952.

The warehouses on Katajanokka, Plate 123, the built-up promontory separating the south from the north harbour, were designed in 1937 by the city architect, Gunnar Taucher. They illustrate the straightforward, somewhat Germanic, functional style that was by this time coming to be accepted in official, as well as in the more advanced private, architectural circles.

12. Helsinki. Stockmann department store. Sigurd Frosterus (1916–30).

113. Turku. *Sanomat* newspaper building. Alvar Aalto (1929): machine hall.
114. Paimio. Tuberculosis sanatorium. Alvar Aalto (1929–33): looking west; patients' balcony wing on left.
115. Paimio. Tuberculosis sanatorium: looking east.

116. Sunila. Cellulose factory. Alvar Aalto (1936–39).

17. Sunila.
Employees'
Housing, Alvar
Aalto (1936–39).

18. Sunila.
Senior employee's
house. Alvar Aalto
(1936–39).

119. Noormarkku. Country house (Villa Mairea). Alvar and Aino Aalto (1939).
120. Nakkila Church. Erkki Huttunen (1937).
121. Turku. Resurrection Chapel. Erik Bryggman (1939): interior.

120

122. Helsinki.
Olympic Stadium.
Yrjö Lindegren
and Toivo
Jäntti (1934–52).

123. Helsinki.
Katajanokka
warehouses.
Gunnar Taucher
(1937).

11 Modern Architecture after 1940

WHEN BUILDING BEGAN AGAIN AFTER THE SECOND WORLD WAR ALVAR
Aalto was the established hero figure of Finnish architecture and the one link
between it and the international architectural scene of which he and his influence
were increasingly part. His first important post-war building, the civic group at
Säynätsalo, exemplifies the qualities for which he was by now widely admired
and which determined the nature of his own very personal contribution to the
rapidly maturing international idiom. It was the outcome of a competition held
in 1949. Before then, after the end of the war in Finland, Aalto had been much
in America, teaching at the Massachusetts Institute of Technology and designing
a dormitory building there (1947–48).

Säynätsalo (see page 85), as a conception, is original and inimitable. It was
built at a time when architects were already finding the puritanism of the early
days of modern architecture, and its dependence on rectilinear forms and a
machine aesthetic, cramping instead of inspiring; and as they faced the problem
of fighting their way out of the narrow channels into which they had allowed it
to lead them, they were encouraged to find that Aalto was already in possession
of the wider, freer territory they were struggling towards. He had reached it by
some route of his own, discovered intuitively, and – what is more – had escaped
in doing so the occasional affectation and obsession with his own solutions that
had limited the influence of Frank Lloyd Wright, an older architect of similarly
heroic stature whose work had something in common with Aalto's in that its
basis was a sense of architecture's organic wholeness. Wright was a great man as
well as a fierce opponent of the worship of technology, but as obstinate as a mule
and with as little chance of progeny.

Aalto, on the other hand, is the prime exemplar of the open mind and has borne in Finland numerous progeny, as we shall see later – but progeny in the most constructive sense; followers who, though they could not have achieved what they have without Aalto's inspiration and example, are far from being imitators of the master. His influence can be seen in much of their work but they have developed in their own way. They take after Aalto, however, in using modern techniques adventurously, idiosyncratically and at the same time humanly, and in reproducing in their work the geometrical vigour and direct relationship between form and materials that Finnish architecture has shown throughout its history.

In spite of its emphasis on the organic, modern Finnish architecture is not anti-scientific; witness Aalto's inventive use of plywood in the design of furniture – so scientifically exploited as to make it virtually a new material. Wood is the material with which his most personal designs are especially associated, and this again is wholly consistent with the way Finland and its landscape are with him and within him whatever he does – a fact that perhaps explains the slight lessening in assurance observable in the buildings he has designed in other countries than Finland.

Birch and pine forests not only clothe Finland's primeval landscape but are the source of the country's industries and the basis of its economy, and in the same way that Saarinen and his associates, when they first broke away from the sterile academic rules and preconceptions at the end of the nineteenth century, sought their inspiration in the log buildings of the Karelian countryside and the richly decorative patterns of the shingled roofs of medieval churches, so virility and virtuosity in the use of wood have become an instinctive and fruitful resource of nearly all the modern Finnish architects. Aalto's own handling of it, though original, is never eccentric; it has a quality of inevitability derived from his craftsmanlike pleasure in perfecting the design of a building component in relation to the job it has to do, at the same time as he engineers its contribution to a coherent whole. His solutions to a design problem, however romantic they may seem, are the outcome of a strictly functional process of analysis.

The critic's inevitable insistence on the organic nature of Finnish architecture in general and Aalto's in particular, and on the inspiration it derives from Finland's testing climate, primitive topography and limited material resources, must not, however, lead him to classify it as regional in any provincial or chauvinistic sense. Nor must he lay too much emphasis on its roots in the soil of Finland. From these may be derived some of the qualities that mark it as recognizably Finnish, but its essential qualities are independent of local allegiances. Aalto and the other Finnish architects are without sentimentality; though in certain ways regionally inspired, they are fully involved in the scientifically orientated international world of architecture.

A somewhat different kind of influence that is important in Finland – more so perhaps than anywhere else – as this account of the development over the centuries of a separate Finnish architecture has had repeatedly to point out, is the stubborn Finnish people's consciousness of their long drawn out struggle to assert and maintain their independence. This cannot be divorced from the nature of the architecture they create. In the case of Aalto himself, his life-span has coincided exactly with the successive struggles and upheavals that have dominated recent Finnish history. He was born (in 1898) at the time of the strictest repression by Imperial Russia and of growing public restiveness because of it; he was a child during the first stirrings of revolution; national independence in 1917 saw the start of his architectural career, and he grew to maturity as an architect just as Finland emerged from the ordeals – emotional as well as material – of the second World War.

Finland had lost to Russia the wealthy eastern province of Karelia, which had not only resulted in severe economic difficulties but had brought half a million refugees trekking into the remaining areas of the country, a number amounting at the time to 12 per cent of the whole population. This created urgent planning and resettlement problems (between 1944 and 1955 Aalto – like Saarinen at a similar stage in his career, after the previous war – became for a time as much a town-planner as an architect, working on plans for expanded industrial settlements at Rovaniemi and elsewhere), and in particular it created housing problems over and above those that inevitably follow a destructive war.

Throughout the 1940s Finland's architectural energies were concentrated on dealing with this and similar problems. In 1949 a national building-loan department (Arava) was set up to help in overcoming the housing shortage. Its work was not always architecturally distinguished and Finnish industrial development was not yet such that it could usefully exploit systematized building techniques, but the experience it offered kept the new generation of Finnish architects well in touch with social realities. Not until the 1950s, however, was the pre-war creativeness of Finnish architecture recaptured, a process assisted perhaps by somewhat less stringent economic conditions – the 1950s were years of intensive industrial growth and in particular of the development of hydro-electric resources, as a result of many new installations, notably at Oulu (where again Aalto had been active as a town-planner) – and it was assisted also by Finland's renewal of contacts with the rest of Europe and America. Finland continued, as it had done in the past, to look to the West culturally, though now compelled to look to the East rather more than to the West economically.

The post-war generation of Finnish architects was largely composed at first of those who had been Aalto's pupils. Later, when one of his pupils of the 1930s, Viljo Rewell (1910–64), had established himself as perhaps the second most influential architect in Finland, it was his office that became the nursery of the growing and rapidly maturing number of able modern architects. Rewell was more of a rationalist and less of a romantic than Aalto, if only in the sense that his best buildings are more rectilinear and less dependent on unexpected

83

sculptural invention – witness his spare and elegant clothing factory at Hanko, to the west of Helsinki (1956).

Characteristic of the architects of this generation is their direct approach to the use of reinforced concrete (along with brick the usual structural material because of the shortage of steel), which has given their buildings a tough individuality – with that of a craftsman's, rather than an industrialist's, relationship to his material – similar to the individuality that has lately shown itself in the modern architecture of Japan; witness especially the most recent work of Aarno Ruusuvuori such as his church at Huutoniemi or his printing works at Tapiola (Plates 175 and 152).

Also characteristic is – as previously – their virtuosity in handling wood; witness the interior of the student restaurant at Otaniemi (Plate 144) by Kaija and Heikki Siren, where the roof and its supporting structures are composed of a multiplicity of wooden struts and ties, fixed together with iron straps and bolts. Again the material is used scientifically, yet with the live muscular quality we are more accustomed to finding in the work of a less self-conscious kind of craftsman, such as a boat-builder.

In spite of the architects' energy and talent, their increasingly sophisticated style of design did not establish itself in Finland without a struggle. The revolt against the academies of forty years before had prepared the ground, and Aalto's increasing international prestige was a powerful weapon, but full public support and intelligent patronage had to be painstakingly worked for. Aalto himself was given no opportunity to design a building in Helsinki the capital (apart from his own pre-war house in the suburb of Munkkiniemi) until 1952, and even this was the result of victory in a competition.

Since then public support has grown, and in Finland architecture is now (along with forestry) a profession to which special prestige is attached. This provides part of the answer to the question that is so often asked about modern Finnish architecture: how is it that a small, geographically remote nation, with limited resources and a relatively brief cultural history, has managed to become, in this field, one of the leading nations of the world, to which the architects of other nations look up and make respectful pilgrimage?

There are other answers too, and one can only think that the explanation of this phenomenon is that it is the cumulative result of several factors, which can perhaps be enumerated as follows. First there is, as already indicated, the presence, influence and international reputation of Alvar Aalto – one cannot but return continually to Aalto's inspiration and example in spite of the fact that in more recent years the range of Finnish architectural activities and the variety of talent available have removed architecture far beyond the capacity of a single genius to determine, Secondly, there is the prestige, already mentioned, accorded to architecture as a social as well as an aesthetic undertaking, and the attention given to it in the press. Thirdly, and closely allied to this, there is the prevalence of the competition system – nearly every major new building is the subject of a competition – which offers big chances to architecturally still uncorrupted youth. The results of competitions, again, are fully reported and discussed in the press.

Fourthly, there is the *youth* of the country: when Finland became independent in 1917 more than one-third of the three million population was under 15 – only one-seventh, incidentally, were town dwellers, but there are many more now. Fifthly, there is the very rapidity of the post-war process of industrialization, which has transformed Finland in a short time from one of the least industrialized countries in Europe and has given a sharp impetus to the evolution of new technical means and resources. Sixthly, there is the discipline imposed and the challenge presented by severe climatic conditions – Finland being, as I observed in the introductory chapter of this book, a land in which the rocks lie very near the surface: a statement that can be understood in more senses than one. And seventhly, there is the intense consciousness, again already referred to, of national identity, which naturally finds expression in architecture.

But inevitably, in appraising Finnish architecture, we find ourselves returning again to its genius for resolving the conflicts that bewilder and frustrate the architects of nearly every other nation. The modern architect inhabits a world of conflict. In every aspect of his profession he is drawn in two opposite directions. He has to discover how to use the new industrialized techniques and yet to evoke human responses; he has also to discover how to combine the international nature of modern architecture – founded on the conception that science knows no political boundaries – with its need to respond to local conditions and cultures. The achievement of the best of the modern Finnish architecture is that it manages to be scientific without being inhuman, regional without being provincial and individual without being whimsical or egocentric.

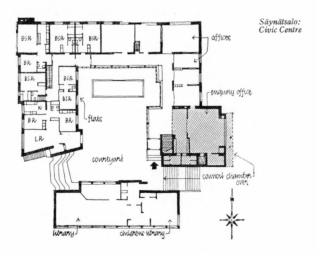

*Säynätsalo:
Civic Centre*

Säynätsalo   This group of civic buildings in central Finland, just south of Jyväskylä
PLATES 124 and   (Aalto's home town) and near where he has his summer cottage at
125   Muuratsalo, was built in 1950–52 (following a competition held in 1949)

85

for a small one-industry town on an island, reached by a long suspension bridge. It is Aalto's most personal work; intimate and idiosyncratic, with an unusual layout directly responsive to the *genius loci*. The various buildings – municipal offices, council chamber, library and officials' residences – are planned round a courtyard which is artificially raised above the surrounding wooded countryside by using the material excavated for the buildings' foundations. Gaps between the buildings allow access to the courtyard – from which they are all entered – by flights of steps, and also allow views towards distant lakes and the penetration of the low northern sun. Materials are dark red brick, wood and copper, and the abruptly varied roof-shapes, seen through closely planted trees, cause the whole group to be absorbed into the rugged landscape and to appear as a romantic intensification of the scene it is set down in.

Helsinki

PLATES 126–141

The Rautatalo (Steel Federation) office building, Plates 126 and 127, in Keskuskatu, one of Helsinki's main shopping streets, was the first building by Aalto to be completed in the capital. It was built in 1953–55, following a competition in 1952. The street façade, with an unusual window layout, which does not in fact reflect the floor-levels within, is framed in copper. There are shops at street level, and between them steps lead up to a large covered interior court containing a café. This is lined with travertine and surrounded by galleries from which the offices are reached. Among the shops is that belonging to Artek, a company that makes and markets some of the best Finnish furniture, glass and textiles, founded by Mme Gullichsen for whom Aalto designed the Villa Mairea – see page 80 and Plate 119.

The National Pensions Institute, by Aalto (competition 1948; completed 1956), occupies a restricted triangular site in the northern part of the city, Plates 128 and 129. Its red-brick buildings, copper-trimmed, step up the slope and enclose a raised courtyard. The canteen, shown in the interior photograph and on the left in the exterior, exemplifies Aalto's decorative inventiveness; note the metal ceiling panels containing heating units and the walls lined with rounded ceramic tiles – invented by Aalto for this occasion and used by him in several buildings subsequently.

The so-called 'House of Culture' (Alvar Aalto, 1958), Plate 130, is a meeting-hall for a number of left-wing political parties and trade unions, also in the northern part of the city but east of the main railway line bisecting it. A high curvilinear wall wraps round an asymmetrical auditorium, seating 1,500, and its foyers and restaurants. The wall, which illustrates Aalto's sculptural proclivities, is made of specially designed wedge-shaped bricks that can conform to any desired curve, convex or concave.

The Enzo-Gutzeit building (Alvar Aalto, 1962), Plate 131, is the headquarters of a wood-pulp and paper corporation. It occupies a prominent position overlooking the south harbour and is seen as part of the view looking north (Plate 76) of the early nineteenth-century waterfront buildings with the Lutheran cathedral rising behind them. To conform, it has been designed to present a horizontal mass, white in colour, but the walling material is hard Carrara marble in contrast to the softer-textured stucco predominating in the neoclassical buildings near by. The façades are heavily modelled, the marble surround of each window being shaped into an angular profile.

The 'Porthania' building of the university (Aarne Ervi, 1957), Plate 132, adjoins the old university area, being sited in Hallituskatu immediately to the west of Engel's library. It houses the faculties of law, mathematics and language and also contains several large auditoria. It was the first building in Helsinki of prestressed, prefabricated reinforced concrete construction, and has some spectacular free-standing staircases. It is faced on the outside with ceramic mosaic.

The Palace Hotel, Plate 133, on the waterfront facing the south harbour (Viljo Rewell and Keijo Petäjä), is a combined hotel and office building completed in 1952 (following a competition held in 1949) to serve as the headquarters for the Olympic Games. On the ground floor are shops and the entrance foyer of the hotel; from the latter lifts serve the hotel bedrooms on the upper floors and the restaurant on the first floor, the intermediate floors containing offices with separate access. The building, which is faced with slabs of reconstructed stone, owes its somewhat austere character partly to the time of economic stringency at which it was built but also to a positive reaction against the romanticism at that time still evident in Aalto's and some other architects' work.

The new building for the Guards' barracks, Plate 134, in Makasiinikatu (a couple of blocks west of the Palace Hotel) is the first instalment, completed in 1961, of a scheme by Viljo Rewell and Heikki Castrén for rebuilding the large section of the barracks – originally a group of neoclassical buildings by Carl Ludwig Engel – that had been destroyed in the war. The photograph shows, on the right, part of the Engel building of 1825, facing on to Kasarmi Square, which survived the bombing – see page 50.

The Meilahti primary school (Viljo Rewell and Osmo Sipari, 1952), Plate 135, in a northern residential district of Helsinki, has an undulating two-storey classroom wing with an assembly hall behind. It has a reinforced concrete frame with panel infilling of brick and was the first Finnish school of this type.

The National Serum Institute, Plate 136, at the northern end of Mannerheimintie (Veli Paatela, 1959) is a range of low laboratory buildings with copper-clad saw-tooth rooflights. The architect was previously one of Aalto's chief assistants and worked with him on the M.I.T. dormitory building in the U.S.A.

The secondary school (Jorma Järvi, 1955) at Kulosaari, an island suburb to the east of Helsinki, on the road to Porvoo, has an assembly hall at its centre, Plate 137, with fixed raking seats, an open wood roof of unusual design and wooden stairs bracketed out from the side wall.

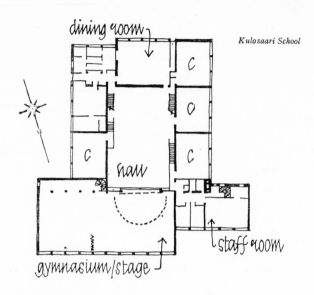

dining room

Kulosaari School

c

o

c

hall

c

gymnasium/stage

staff room

These lead to the upper floor classrooms. Järvi, who died in 1962 at the early age of 54, was a pioneer of modern Finnish school architecture. Besides a number of schools he designed the Helsinki Olympic swimming stadium, completed in 1952.

The Marski Hotel (Einari Teräsvirta, 1961), Plate 138, in Mannerheimintie in the very centre of the city, exemplifies the competent quality of much of Helsinki's city-scale street architecture and its frequent use of copper trim. Its plain ribbon-windowed façade is enlivened by well-disposed lettering. The building contains office as well as hotel accommodation. The hotel interiors are by Ilmari Tapiovaara. Teräsvirta was also the architect of the Students' Union Library at Töölö, Helsinki (1955).

In the island suburb of Lauttasaari (Swedish Drumsö), west of the city, the parish church (Keijo Petäjä, 1958), Plate 139, occupies a paved platform in the centre of the island on the axis of its main avenue. The U-shaped group of buildings, comprising church, parish hall and parish offices, is approached by a wide flight of steps and encloses a courtyard in which stands a slender detached bell-tower (its base is on the left in the photograph). The church's interior designer was Ilmari Tapiovaara.

Also in Lauttasaari is the highly sophisticated courtyard house (in Takaniementie) designed in 1960 by Toivo Korhonen and Jaakko Laapotti for the former's own occupation, Plate 140. All the living quarters are at the same level, raised above a basement containing a swimming bath and a garage, and surround a glass-enclosed garden.

The same planning principle was followed by the same two architects in a group of small houses in the Espoo area, about six miles southwest of Helsinki, built in 1959, Plate 141. One- and two-storey houses, in parallel rows, are planned round small enclosed gardens.

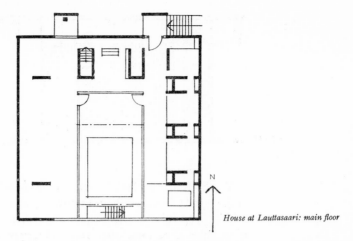

House at Lauttasaari: main floor

Other interesting housing in the Helsinki suburbs includes flats in Merimiehenkatu by Aarno Ruusuvuori (1962), flats in Herttoniemi by Osmo Sipari (1957), flats at Lauttasaari by Toivo Korhonen (1960) and houses at Lauttasaari by Keijo Petäjä (1957). Other modern buildings in Helsinki worth the visitor's attention and not already mentioned include the neurosurgical clinic in Töölö (Veli Paatela, 1957), the Workers' Institute, Helsinginkatu (Aulis Blomstedt, 1959) – an extension of a 1927 building by Taucher – the Olympia Hotel, with sports hall, restaurant and shops, in the Kallio district (Niilo Pulkka, 1961), a small studio theatre built on to the National Theatre (Kaija and Heikki Siren, 1954), an old people's home at Espoo for the Salvation Army (Jonas Cedercreutz, 1964) and Aalto's own office in Munkkiniemi (1956), a white-walled L-shaped building on changing levels enclosing an amphitheatre-shaped garden.

Helsinki: Otaniemi

PLATES 142–144

On a wooded peninsula across the bay to the west of Helsinki, in the rural district of Espoo, is Otaniemi, the site of the rapidly growing Institute of Technology, where all the institutes of higher technical education are being gathered together, many of them (including the school of architecture) having been transferred here from older buildings in the city. The buildings at Otaniemi are laid out according to a plan made by Aalto in 1949. The main building (1964), Plate 142, is also by Aalto and shows a return to his earlier, more expressionist, style. It houses several faculties, the central administration and auditoria, the largest auditorium being contained in the tall block, curved in plan and triangular in section, seen in the photograph. The foyers open on to raised terraces partly enclosed by the wings of the building.

The several blocks of student living accommodation (Heikki Siren and M. Melakari), a sports hall (Aalto), used for the Olympic Games, and a students' restaurant (Kaija and Heikki Siren), Plate 144, were all built in 1952. The interior of the restaurant, illustrated here, is typically expressive and vigorous in its use of wood construction.

R

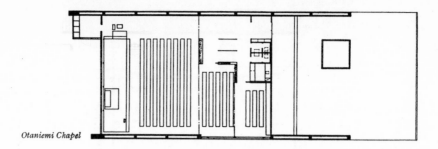

Otaniemi Chapel

Also by Kaija and Heikki Siren is the chapel, Plate 143, half hidden in the woods. This was built in 1956–57 after a competition had been held in 1954. It is designed as part of its sylvan setting and has a simple rectangular plan, a one-pitch roof and a gravelled, tree-planted courtyard containing an open wooden bell-tower. The whole east wall of the chapel is of glass, allowing the view into the depths of the wood to serve as a reredos behind the altar.

Helsinki:
Tapiola
PLATES 145–152

Just south of Otaniemi is Tapiola, the satellite town begun in 1952 and now (1966) on the point of reaching its planned final population of 17,000. It was founded by a number of welfare and housing organizations who jointly established the Asuntosäätiö building society, a non profit-making organization, to plan and finance the new town. A competition for the layout was won by Aarne Ervi. It consists of three residential neighbourhoods of approximately equal size, each with a mixture of terrace houses and tall flats built to a fairly low overall density among trees and winding roads. They are grouped round an administrative and shopping centre, sited alongside an open space containing a lake with a secondary school nearby. All the dwellings are supplied with heating, hot water and electricity from one central power station.

Aarne Ervi was also the architect of the buildings comprising the

Typical flats in block at Tapiola
(Plate 148)

main centre: a thirteen-storey tower block of administrative offices with a restaurant on the top floor, Plate 145, linked with a tree-planted square, surrounded by shops, Plate 146. This again was the subject of a competition, held in 1954; the buildings were completed in 1961.

About a dozen different architects have designed houses and flats at Tapiola, and the standard both of architecture and of landscaping is, with very few exceptions, high. Four typical examples are illustrated here: a terrace of studio houses (Aulis Blomstedt, 1956), Plate 147, each with a double-height studio with a gallery across one end; a four-storey block of flats (Viljo Rewell, 1954), Plate 148, raised on columns and constructed of prefabricated reinforced concrete units; a quadrangle surrounded by flats (Viljo Rewell, 1958), Plate 149, and one of a row of fairly luxurious houses (Kaija and Heikki Siren, 1959), Plate 150. These make use of a sloping site to raise the main floor well above road level, at which level there is a double garage with the living-room extending over it and terminating in a south-facing balcony.

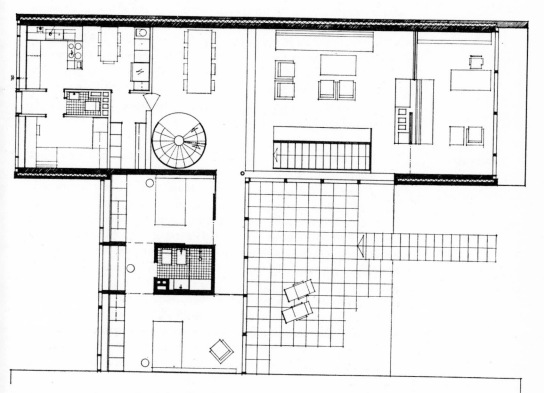

House at Tapiola (Plate 150)

The secondary school near the main centre, Plate 151, is by Jorma Järvi (1960), a single-storey building planned in three wings: two class-room wings with hexagonal libraries and lecture halls branching from them, and an assembly hall wing with a high parabolic roof.

Tapiola is intended eventually to provide local employment for 30 per cent of its inhabitants; at present this is largely limited to service industries and a few offices, but a recent addition is a printing works (Aarno Ruusuvuori, 1964), Plate 152, occupying a square reinforced concrete building with a roof suspended from four exposed central columns.

Turku
Swedish Åbo
PLATES 153 and
154

The modern University of Turku, on a hill east of the cathedral, consists of a large compactly planned group of buildings surrounding a courtyard. The Library, Plate 153, which closes the west side of the courtyard, was added in 1954 (architect, Aarne Ervi). It is entered at an upper level, with two floors of bookstacks below and two floors of reading-rooms, seen in the photograph, above. It has a reinforced concrete frame.

On the southern side of the river, facing across it towards the modern centre of Turku, is the municipal theatre (Risto-Veikko Luukonen and Helmer Stenros, 1962), Plate 154. It was the subject of a competition and is intended to be the first of a group of civic buildings. The theatre is dominated by the high square block of the stage tower, clad in copper – a material (always in fashion among modern Finnish architects) also used for the columns and wall mullions of the upper-level foyer which projects from the side of the auditorium towards the river. The building is notable for its crisp assured detail, which contrasts with the somewhat heavier exterior treatment of the same architects' later municipal theatre at Kuopio – see Plate 176.

Tampere
PLATES 155–157

The most distinguished modern building in Tampere (again the subject of a competition) is the Institute of Social Sciences (Toivo Korhonen and Jaakko Laapotti, 1962), designed as the nucleus of a future university, Plates 155 and 156. It is cruciform in shape, with lecture halls in the centre of the main wing and other rooms that need high ceilings, such as refectories and libraries, at either end of it. Teaching, study and administrative rooms occupy the transverse wing, on two floors. The building has (unusually in Finland) a steel frame and precast wall panels with a marble aggregate. The roof of the main lecture hall is suspended from beams exposed on the outside of the building. These can be seen in the photograph, which shows the west façade and the windows of the refectory. This and the other main rooms at first-floor level, including the large lecture hall, are reached by the broad staircase shown in the other photograph. The interior designer was Esko Pajamies.

On the south-east edge of the city, off the road to Messukylä, is the general hospital (Helamaa and Martikainen, 1961) with a multi-storey ward block and lower treatment wings standing among fir trees.

Further out from Tampere, about eight miles from the city in the same direction, is the Vatiala cemetery with a reinforced concrete chapel (1962) by Viljo Rewell in a well-landscaped setting of lawns and trees, Plate 157. The building, the subject of a competition, contains a large and a small chapel separated by a hall in which congregations can gather between services. The large chapel has a parabolic roof covered with copper.

Also in Tampere are the Sampola school (Penttilä and Virta, 1962), notable for its spacious staircase halls and its auditorium with raking floor, the Kaleva church (Reima Pietilä; competition held 1959, but still under construction at the time of writing), with an odd rhomboid plan formed by curved wall panels of reinforced concrete, and, in a pine forest on the edge of the town, an unusual summer theatre, built of logs with an auditorium that revolves to bring the audience opposite different stages and to allow the lake shore and the natural forest to serve as scenery.

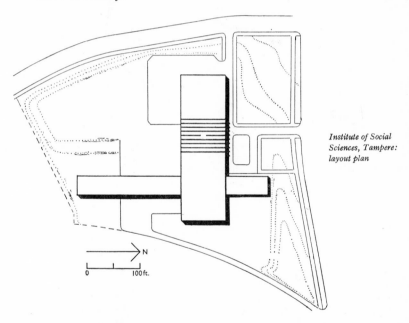

Institute of Social Sciences, Tampere: layout plan

Jyväskylä
PLATES 158–161

This town in mid-Finland has a long educational tradition, having been the first place to institute teaching in the Finnish language in 1858. Here is the central teachers' training college for the whole of Finland, founded in 1863, whose nineteenth-century buildings, now providing students' living accommodation, have been supplemented by a range of new buildings by Alvar Aalto, the winner of a competition held in 1950. Construction began in 1953 and has continued in stages since. Aalto's buildings, mostly in his favourite hard red brick, are arranged

93

Teachers' Training College, Jyväskylä

round three sides of a long narrow sports field (bottom of plan on facing page). On the east (see Plate 159) are the staff refectory (shown in close-up in Plate 161), the students' refectory and a dormitory; on the north the library and a primary school where the students gain teaching experience; on the west a gymnasium and a swimming bath. At the north-east corner is the main teaching building with a large entrance foyer on the axis of the road by which the college is approached through its wooded grounds – the road being an extension of the main street of the town. This foyer, which leads to a large auditorium, has on its left a glass wall dramatically revealing the forest scenery outside and on its right a long staircase hall (Plate 160) serving smaller auditoria, laboratories and studios. This hall exemplifies Aalto's skilful and imaginative handling of interior space.

Also by Aalto, and close to the grounds of the training college, is the Central Finnish Museum (1961), a modest white-walled building overlooking a steep grassy bank. Jyväskylä hospital, which serves as the general hospital for all central Finland (Jonas Cedercreutz and Helge Railo, 1950–54), Plate 158, has a ten-storey central block with radiating wings and three independent tower blocks for staff housing.

Lahti
PLATES 162–165

At the junction of two of Lahti's main streets is the last building completed by Viljo Rewell before he died in 1964: a bank building, Plate 162, designed, like most of his later work, with his partner Heikki Castrén. The main banking hall, Plate 163, is on the first floor, reached by escalators, with clerestory lighting along one side and surrounded on the other sides by galleries giving access to offices.

On the edge of Lahti is the cemetery, with a simple white-walled chapel (Niilo Pulkka, 1958), Plate 164, well placed among trees and lawns, and in the eastern part of the town is a large private-enterprise housing development (Olli Vahtera, 1962–65), Plate 165. Blocks of flats surround an open space which dips down from a main road along which a series of identical high blocks is arranged in echelon.

Vaasa
PLATES 166 and 167

The whole of one side of the central square in this harbour town on the Gulf of Bothnia is occupied by a large commercial redevelopment (Viljo Rewell and Heikki Castrén, 1963), Plate 166. At present it is somewhat too large in scale to accord with its surroundings, but when further redevelopment takes place this defect should rectify itself since the square is big enough to take buildings of this height. A long seven-storey block of shops and offices faces the square, the shops being on two levels, the upper level reached by an open deck. Beneath the deck is a way through to an inner pedestrian square, shown in the photograph, enclosed by single-storey shops and another high block containing offices and flats.

Between Vaasa and Seinäjoki is a milk depot and processing plant (Matti Mäkinen, 1964) planned round a planted forecourt and exemplifying Finnish industrial architecture at its best: Plate 167.

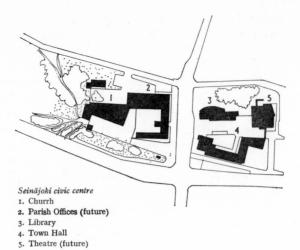

Seinäjoki civic centre
1. Churrh
2. **Parish Offices (future)**
3. Library
4. Town Hall
5. Theatre (future)

Seinäjoki

PLATES 168 and
169

This growing industrial town in the flat plain of Ostrobothnia, south-east of Vaasa, is equipping itself with an ambitious civic centre by Alvar Aalto, who was the winner of a competition, held in 1952, for the church only. This was completed in 1960, and while it was building there was another competition, also won by Aalto, for a comprehensive group of civic buildings, the first two of which, a town-hall and a library, were completed by 1964. There is also to be a theatre, and a range of parish offices forming a square facing the west end of the church. The square will have a stepped floor surface designed so that it can serve as an outdoor extension of the congregation space within, the west wall of the church sliding open to link the two spaces. Neither of the two additional buildings has yet been started, and the whole group suffers from being bisected by a main road. It is also at present somewhat detached from the town. This will no doubt be remedied as the intervening land is built up, but according to Aalto's plan another main road at right-angles will still intervene between the civic centre and the town.

The separate buildings demonstrate Aalto's imaginative sense of geometrical relationships. The town-hall in particular, which has walls faced with Aalto's favourite rounded tiles (see under the National Pensions Institute, Helsinki, page 86) in a dark blue colour, highly glazed, is full of inventive devices. The main floor is raised up and the staircase hall at street level is approached through a colonnade beneath it. Rising through the main floor is the triangular upper part of the council chamber. From the pedestrian square at the other side of the building – between it and the library – the upper level can be reached directly by climbing a stepped, grass-grown slope, and from there another outside stair, in a slit between two tile-faced walls, leads still higher to the council chamber's public gallery.

Vuoksenniska

PLATES 170 and 171

In a loosely scattered industrial area surrounding the town of Imatra (see page 71), in south-eastern Finland, right on the Russian frontier, Aalto has built another church at Vuoksenniska, completed in 1959, Plates 170 and 171. It is sited among trees, and the tower has been given a distinctive outline so that it can be easily identified among the many factory chimneys which also rise above the trees and with which it cannot compete in height. The church, which has white plastered walls and copper roofs, has an ingeniously complex plan-shape based on the need to enlarge or reduce its seating capacity at will and enable it to serve various purposes. There are three areas, each with one straight and one rounded side wall, separated by sliding partitions. The first, containing also the altar and pulpit, can serve as a chapel for wedding and funeral services and the like. By opening the partitions space can be made for successively larger congregations, and the two outer areas can be used separately, with the partitions closed, for social purposes.

Also at Vuoksenniska, compactly planned across a sloping site, is a secondary school by Jaako Kontio and Kalle Räike, two architects who worked with Aalto on the church.

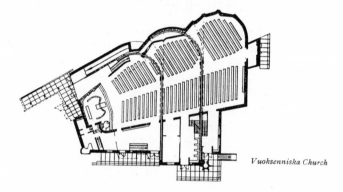

Vuoksenniska Church

Savonlinna

PLATE 172

This town, set among the waterways of the Saimaa lake system in south-eastern Finland, is architecturally most notable for its medieval castle (Olavinlinna – see page 22). It also has a modest but very neatly designed public library (Maija Suurla and Kaisa Harjanne, 1964), with white walls and copper fascia, set on a rocky eminence and reached by winding pathways. The slope of the ground has been used to provide a part lower storey beneath the angled windows of the main reading-room.

Hyvinkää

PLATES 173 and 174

On rocky, tree-planted ground near the centre of this rapidly growing town about 28 miles north of Helsinki is a church (Aarno Ruusuvuori, 1961) of unusual triangular outline. As is usual, it was the subject of a competition, and seats 630 with another 60 in the organ and choir loft. It also contains a parish hall seating 200 which is placed above the entrance vestibule and can be opened into the upper part of the church to serve as a gallery. The building has a rhomboidal plan divided from corner to corner so that the church itself, occupying half the area, is

S

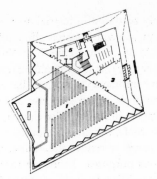

Hyvinkää Church
1. Nave
2. Sanctuary
3. Entrance vestibule
4. Cloakroom and stairs to gallery
5. Vestry

triangular in plan. It is also triangular in section, rising to a peak in the centre of the building. The other half is also triangular in section but not so high, allowing clerestory lighting into the church above the parish hall-gallery. The altar is placed against one of the outside walls so that it is seen at an angle from the entrance and when approached down the aisle between the seats. The building is of reinforced concrete with the long sloping ribs filled in with glass or precast concrete slabs.

Also at Hyvinkää is a school by Keijo Petäjä (1960).

Huutoniemi

PLATE 175

A later church by the same architect as the church at Hyvinkää (Aarno Ruusuvuori) was completed in this village near Vaasa in 1964. Again it is wholly in reinforced concrete, but is treated in a more sober and less aggressively angular fashion. This church achieves a calm distinction with no other material than grey board-marked concrete walls used with some geometrical subtlety. The building, containing also a double layer of parish rooms, is planned round a courtyard, the entrance to which can be seen in the photograph with the church to the left of it and the belfry to the right. On the far side of the church is a terrace of clergy houses, also in reinforced concrete.

Kuopio

PLATE 176

The munciipal theatre at Kuopio is by the same architects as the theatre at Turku (see Plate 154): Risto-Veikko Luukonen and Helmer Stenros. It was built in 1964 and has a somewhat stolid concrete-mullioned façade but inside a successful first-floor foyer with an open wooden ceiling, shown here.

Rovaniemi

PLATE 177

This newly developed industrial centre in the far north – almost on the Arctic Circle – is the administrative capital of Finnish Lapland. The town was severely damaged by German troops in 1944. Rebuilding has followed a plan drawn up by Alvar Aalto. It is an important communications centre, especially for long-distance bus routes, and has a bus terminus incorporating a small hotel and restaurant, by Niilo Pulkka, Pekka Rajala and Kaarlo Leppänen, completed in 1959 (competition 1956). The windows are triple-glazed to protect the interior against the extreme cold. The sculpturally shaped upper walls are faced with wood boarding.

24. Säynätsalo. Civic Centre. Alvar Aalto (1952): steps up to courtyard; council chamber
     beyond.
25. Säynätsalo. Civic Centre: the library.

126. Helsinki. Rautatalo office building. Alvar Aalto (1955): street façade.

27.   Helsinki. Rautatalo office building: interior court.

128. Helsinki. National Pensions Institute. Alvar Aalto (1956).
129. Helsinki. National Pensions Institute: canteen.
130. Helsinki. 'House of Culture.' Alvar Aalto (1958).

128

129

131. Helsinki. Enzo-Gutzeit building. Alvar Aalto (1962).
132. Helsinki University. 'Porthania' building. Aarne Ervi (1957).
133. Helsinki. Palace Hotel. Viljo Rewell and Keijo Petäjä (1952).
134. Helsinki. Guards' barracks. Viljo Rewell and Heikki Castrén (1961).

133

134

135. Helsinki. Meilahti primary school. Viljo Rewell and Osmo Sipari (1952).
136. Helsinki. National Serum Institute. Veli Paatela (1959).
137. Helsinki. Kulosaari secondary school. Jorma Järvi (1955): assembly hall.

138.

138. Helsinki. Marski Hotel. Einari Teräsvirta (1961).
139. Helsinki. Lauttasaari Church. Keijo Petäjä (1958).
140. Helsinki. Courtyard house in Lauttasaari. Toivo Korhonen and Jaakko Laapotti (1960).
141. Helsinki: Espoo. Housing. Toivo Korhonen and Jaakko Laapotti (1959).

139

142

143

142. Helsinki: Otaniemi. Institute of Technology, main building. Alvar Aalto (1964).
143. Helsinki: Otaniemi. Chapel. Kaija and Heikki Siren (1957).
144. Helsinki: Otaniemi. Students' Restaurant. Kaija and Heikki Siren (1952).

145.   Helsinki: Tapiola. Administrative centre. Aarne Ervi (1961).
146.   Helsinki: Tapiola. Shopping square in main centre. Aarne Ervi (1961).
147.   Helsinki: Tapiola. Studio houses. Aulis Blomstedt (1956).

148. Helsinki: Tapiola. Flats. Viljo Rewell (1954).

149. Helsinki:
Tapiola. Flats.
Viljo Rewell
(1958).

150. Helsinki:
Tapiola. House.
Kaija and Heikki
Siren (1959).

151. Helsinki: Tapiola. Secondary school. Jorma Järvi (1960).
152. Helsinki: Tapiola. Printing works. Aarno Ruusuvuori (1964).

153.   Turku. University library. Aarne Ervi (1954).
154.   Turku. Municipal Theatre. Risto-Veikko Luukonen and Helmer Stenros (1962).

155. Tampere. Institute of Social Sciences. Toivo Korhonen and Jaakko Laapotti (1962).
156. Tampere. Institute of Social Sciences. Toivo Korhonen and Jaakko Laapotti (1962): main stair.
157. Tampere: Vatiala. Cemetery Chapel. Viljo Rewell (1962).
158. Jyväskylä. General Hospital. Jonas Cedercreutz and Helge Railo (1954).

158

159. Jyväskylä. Teachers' Training College. Alvar Aalto (1953–64).
160. Jyväskylä. Teachers' Training College: staircase hall in main building.
161. Jyväskylä. Teachers' Training College: staff refectory.

162. Lahti.
Kansallis-Osake
Bank. Viljo
Rewell and
Heikki Castrén
(1964).

163. Lahti.
Kansallis-Osake
Bank: banking
hall.

64. Lahti.
Cemetery Chapel.
Niilo Pulkka
(1958)

65. Lahti.
Housing.
Ili Vahtera
(1962–65).

166. Vaasa. Shops and Offices, central square. Viljo Rewell and Heikki Castrén (1963).
167. Vaasa. Milk Depot. Matti Mäkinen (1964).
168. Seinäjoki. Civic Centre. Alvar Aalto (1960–64): town hall on left; church in background.
169. Seinäjoki. Civic Centre: entrance of town hall.

166

167

173. Hyvinkää Church.
Aarno Ruusuvuori (1961).
174. Hyvinkää Church: interior.
175. Huutoniemi Church.
Aarno Ruusuvuori (1964).
176. Kuopio. Municipal Theatre. Risto-Veikko Luukonen and Helmer Stenros (1964): first floor foyer.

177. Rovaniemi. Bus station. Niilo Pulkka, Pekka Rajala and Kaarlo Leppänen (1959).

Bibliography

The following is a short list of books on Finnish architecture written wholly in English or with some of the text or captions translated into English. The author of the present volume is indebted in some degree to all of them for facts, dates and other information, though the opinions he expresses and his interpretation of events are his own; so is the responsibility for any errors that may be discovered in these pages.

Alvar Aalto. Girsberger, Zurich, 1963. The architect's complete works illustrated and described. Text in German, English and French.

Art Treasures of Medieval Finland. Otava, Helsinki, no date. Picture book (photographs by István Rácz) chiefly concerned with wall-paintings and sculpture but with notes at the end on the churches in which they are found. These are in English; so is the short introduction. Captions to the pictures in Finnish only.

Christ-Janer, Albert. **Eliel Saarinen.** University of Chicago Press, 1948. Illustrated biography.

Finland's Most Beautiful Churches. K. J. Gummerus, Jyväskylä, 1962. Picture book with introduction (by Antero Sinisalo) and captions in Finnish, Swedish, English and German. Architectural notes at the end in Finnish only.

Helsinki Architectural Guide. Otava, 1963. Illustrated pocket guide to old and modern buildings, compiled by the Finnish Architectural Museum. Introduction (by Otto Meurman) and notes on the buildings in Finnish, Swedish and English.

T

Neuenschwander, E. and C., **Alvar Aalto and Finnish Architecture.** Architectural Press, London, 1954. Text in German, English and French.

Wickberg, Nils Erik. **Finnish Architecture.** Otava, Helsinki, 1959. Picture book with short text giving historical background. The best general account. Wholly in English.

The best guide-books in English are the **Finland** volume in the Nagel Travel Guide series, published in Geneva (latest edition 1964), and **The Travellers' Guide to Finland,** by Sylvie Nickels (Jonathan Cape, London, 1965).

The Photographs

The following are the copyright owners and photographers of the plates comprising the illustration pages.

J. M. Richards: Plates 2, 3, 4, 10, 20, 21, 22, 23, 27, 28, 30, 31, 34, 36, 37, 40, 42, 43, 45, 46, 47, 48, 49, 50, 51, 52, 53, 54, 57, 61, 62, 64, 65, 67, 69, 71, 72, 74, 75, 77, 78, 79, 80, 81, 82, 83, 84, 85, 86, 87, 90, 91, 94, 95, 97, 98, 99, 102, 103, 104, 110, 111, 117, 118, 131, 143, 145, 146, 149, 150, 151, 154, 155, 157, 159, 161, 162, 164, 165, 168, 169, 170, 172, 173, 174.

Museum of Finnish Architecture, Helsinki (Asko Salokorpi): Plates 1, 89, 92, 106; (Wickberg): Plate 6; (Air Forces): Plate 63; (Karhumäki): Plate 70; (Roos): Plates 76, 96, 105, 116; (F. Runeberg): Plate 88; (Iffland): Plates 93, 123; (Havas): Plates 101, 122, 126, 127, 128, 129, 130, 133, 135, 136, 141, 144, 147, 148, 156, 177; (N. Wasastjerna): Plate 112; (G. Welin): Plates 113, 119; (V. Maarela): Plate 134; (Pietinen): Plates 138, 152; (Petäjä): Plate 139; (Simo Rista): Plate 140; (Ingervo): Plates 142, 160; (Airaksinen): Plate 166; (Mäkinen): Plate 167; (Julkunen): Plate 175; and Plates 8, 9, 11, 13, 15, 16, 18, 19, 24, 26, 29, 73, 108, 109, 114, 115, 120, 121, 125, 137.

K. J. Gummerus, Jyväskylä (G. Welin): Plates 7, 12, 14, 17, 25, 32, 33, 35, 39, 41, 43, 44, 55, 56, 100, 105, 171.

National Museum of Finland: Plates 58, 59, 60.

Town Museum, Turku: Plates 66, 68.

Hämeenlinna Museum: Plate 5.

Albin Aaltonen: Plate 38.

Aarne Ervi: Plates 132, 153.

Kansallis-Osake Bank, Lahti: Plate 163.

Municipal Theatre, Kuopio (Hämäläinen): Plate 176.

Five of the plans reproduced in the text are from originals supplied by the Museum of Finnish Architecture in Helsinki. For permission to reproduce the others acknowledgement is due to the Otava Publishing Co., Helsinki (publishers of Nils Erik Wickberg's *Finnish Architecture*), the Architectural Press, Ltd., London (publishers of E. and C. Neuenschwander's *Alvar Aalto and Finnish Architecture* and of *The Architectural Review*), Architectural Design, London, Nordisk Rotogravyr, Stockholm (publishers of *Nya Kyrkor i Skandinavien*) and the various architects concerned.

Index

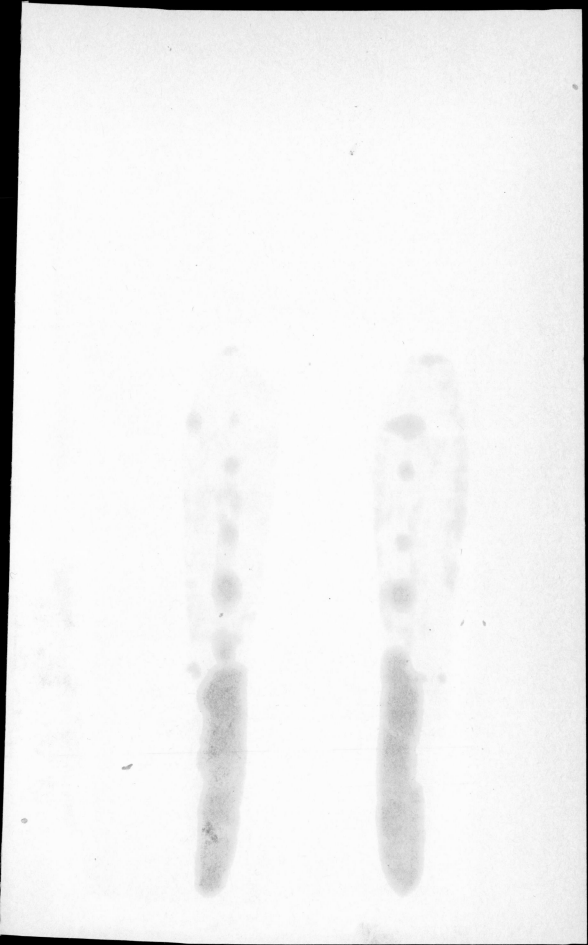